D1253902

TRANSITION

TRANSITION

Essays

on Contemporary Literature

by

EDWIN MUIR

NEW YORK THE VIKING PRESS MCMXXVI

MANUFACTURED IN THE UNITED STATES OF AMERICA
BY THE VAIL-BALLOU PRESS, INC., BINGHAMTON, N. Y.

To

FRANCIS GEORGE SCOTT

PREFACE

THE things with which it is most essential that
the critic should deal are the things of the present:
the books which are being written, the books
which might be written, the tendencies which have
not still found a decisive direction—the forming
body of literature to which his services, if he has
any, will be of immediate and palpable use. But
these are also, unfortunately, the things of which
it is most difficult to write. We are as much the
children of the works of our age as they are of us;
we are part of them, and yet we must pass judgment on them. As a matter of fact we do judge
them, involuntarily or deliberately. We have reactions to them, and then opinions about them.
These opinions transpire in conversation; they
rarely are allowed the publicity of the printed
word. A rash action may occasionally be useful;
and it is in this belief that I have written these

essays on figures whom a later age will judge or will forget.

A true judgment can only be passed by one who has a grasp of all the aspects of the case. In the case of contemporary literature we can be witnesses, defendants, or partisans; we can be nothing more. Accordingly my task has not been one of valuation; valuation can only come when this age itself is judged by a later generation. The most I have attempted, then, has been to understand the aims of the writers I have treated, to point out their merits and limitations without much employment of the comparative method which must be used in coming to any definitive criticism. But what I have done I have done seriously, thinking it right to treat my subjects with as much consideration as if they were dead. This approach has, moreover, the advantage of novelty, for the tendency to treat everything contemporary as if it were not quite genuine is almost universal, and well-nigh unavoidable. This tendency has its virtues, but they are not peculiarly critical ones, and I have tried to avoid them.

The writers I have dealt with are those who

seem to be influencing the development of literature. The older writers and the more conservative of the young I have omitted; their work presents few problems; they may be left to the appreciation of their age. Others, though within the scope of my survey, I have omitted for different reasons. Among these the chief are Mr. Sacheverell Sitwell and Mr. Edmund Blunden, both of whom I admire, but neither of whom has yet, it seems to me, written the work upon which ultimately he will be judged.

Certain of these essays have appeared in *The Nation, The Nation and the Athenæum, The Calendar of Letters,* and *The New Republic.* To the editors of all of them my thanks and acknowledgments are due.

E. M.

Montrose, Scotland.

CONTENTS

INTRODUCTORY: THE ZEIT GEIST

~ I ~

INTRODUCTORY: THE ZEIT GEIST

FOR some time it has been a habit of criticism to
be concerned with the spirit of the age. Books
are praised because they enshrine it, or condemned
because they do not. No doubt this tendency is
a good one; yet a considerable difficulty stands in
its way: that about the spirit of the age it is almost impossible to make an incontestable assertion. We do not know its attributes, nor how it
operates and to what end, nor why it is what it is;
we only know that it is. We cannot tell in which
of our contemporaries it is most essentially represented; whether it is more in Mr. Lawrence than
in Mr. Strachey, whether Miss Sitwell has it or
Mr. Eliot, or whether Mr. Joyce is its true
prophet. Regarding it romantically we might be
tempted to think of it as a force of immense resources, but blind, which throws out parts of itself

3

experimentally in various directions to discover in which it will find its greatest satisfaction.

Yet subjectively, in our experience, we feel it in quite a different way. We feel it as a thing pressing in upon us, a force against which we can never be prepared, for we do not know its strength, its attributes, or the means by which it operates. The writer will express these attributes in works of art, but he can never define them; and when he tries to do so he will fall, as Mr. Lawrence has done in his didactic writings, into half-truth and unintelligibility. In any case he will not feel like a reed through which the spirit of the age blows; that theory of the Zeit Geist will be refuted for him by his ever-present struggle to impose form upon his material.

When a force determining men's lives is indefinable, inescapable, and overpowering, it will arouse hostility in those who realize its power, and this hostility will be the more intense the more complete the realization. A man who apprehends the power of the age will regard himself as its enemy; like Milton, Swift, Blake, Wordsworth, Shelley and a host of other writers, he will show a

4

distaste almost grotesque for contemporary habitudes of thought. This hostility is in certain writers inevitable; it is in effect a testing of the age by itself, an assaying process from which, its deceptions and fashions burned away, the age emerges in greater purity. For all great writers are of their time, though they sometimes think of themselves as outside and against it; and when they attain expression in art the age is interrogating itself, is being differentiated for the purpose of self-realization. Without this hostility against itself the spirit of no age could come to realization; it would remain undifferentiated and unawakened; it could never be objectified, for all objectification implies separation.

And in the greater number of its writers the spirit of an age is never objectified. For the law of mediocrity holds in literature as in ordinary life; the majority of writers accept fashion blindly, never feel the abnormal need to question, are either satisfied with things as they seem, or else are content with a mood of wonder which cannot goad them beyond itself. This is a fact neither to be astonished at nor deplored, but simply to be accepted as inevitable. Writers of this ineradicable order are not necessarily popular; they may have a regard for art; they are sometimes within their limitations sincere; but their decisive limitation is that habitually they speak out of the Zeit Geist as if they were speaking in their sleep. All the thoughts, attitudes, phrases, techniques of the Zeit Geist crowd into their minds and emerge again with an individual twist, it is true, for personality can never be completely abnegated, but without a single fundamental question having been addressed to them. Works produced in this way are immediately understood by all those who are in the stream of the same Zeit Geist. They are understood as *Lalla Rookh* was at a time when Shelley was scarcely known at all, or where known was despised. This comprehension is complete and immediate because writers of this order never question the premises of the age, and because to question premises is always an unfamiliar and unwelcome process. The mark of these writers is that they accept the spirit of the age both consciously and unconsciously; their conscious is accordingly a mere passive reflection of a

6

general unconscious, and is incapable of being turned back into that unconscious, to discover and objectify what is there. They are mere expressions of the thing of which as artists they should be the contemplators. If they have enthusiasm it is not their enthusiasm, if disillusion, not their disillusion, if thoughts, not their thoughts. These are manifestations of a literary fashion, and it is in the essential nature of fashion to blind us to its meaning and the causes from which it springs; to everything, in fact, except the inevitability of the conformity it demands.

There are two ways in which the writer may avoid being assimilated by the age; one is by struggling with it, the other is by escape. Both imply an intense apprehension of the spirit of the age, and both are in greater or less measure salutary, for even by escape the writer maintains his personality intact. But it is he who wrestles with the age who finally justifies both it and himself; for if it oppresses the writer the spirit of the age has also something of incalculable value to give him, which only by it can be given. It not only presents him with a new resistance, unlike that

7

presented by any other period; it gives him a new
inspiration, once the resistance has been vitally
pierced. If, ignoring his age, a writer turns to
past literature for his stimulus, he will find that
the resistance is not sufficient to evoke his full
powers, that try as he may the urgency and immediacy which are the signs in art that the theme
has not merely been chosen but destined, will remain absent from his work. In theory he may
be apparently right; he may justly hold that only
what is permanent is great; yet his orientation to
the problem will be completely erroneous, for the
good writer is not concerned with the things which
in literature have been proved permanent, but
rather with the things in his age and his experience which have not been so proved, to which
by realizing and objectifying them he may give
permanence. What we recognize as the Zeit Geist
of a past age is that part of it which in this way
has been objectified. What we feel as the contemporary Zeit Geist, on the other hand, is a
raw potentiality whose crystallizations in art are
the less clearly recognizable by us the more completely we are under the influence of that potenti-

ality. This blindness about itself is not peculiar
to our age. It is the fate of every age of transition. To the intelligentsia a hundred years ago
the spirit of the age was not represented by Wordsworth, Coleridge, Keats and Shelley, but rather by
Campbell, Moore, and *The Edinburgh Review.*
It is true, the intelligentsia have no power over
us as soon as the age which produced them has
passed, but while they are contemporary they are
the chief moulders of opinion, and have incalculable power, the infinite power of suggestion.
In the modern world the power most solidly ob-
noxious to the artist is not the public but the intelligentsia.

The thesis that the writer who most completely
expresses the spirit of the age is he who is consciously against it is less paradoxical when it is
put in different terms; and if it were said that
to a sincere or original spirit life must always be
more difficult than it is to the mediocre or the
fashionable, the agreement would be general. It
is the almost hypnotic power of suggestion which
contemporary modes of thought, hopes, assumptions, desires cast upon us, that prevents our ad-

mitting readily this particular application of a
generally admitted truth. Nothing is more amaz-
ing in our time, for instance, than the amiability
of literary men towards one another. Dozens of
intelligent critics have not scrupled to call Mr.
de la Mare a great writer; Mr. Chesterton has ac-
corded the same title to Mr. Squire, and Mr.
Strachey, of all people, has bracketed Shakespeare and Mr. Eliot together, evidently as poets
of the same quality. Politeness cannot account
for such happenings; it would be perfectly satisfied with the acknowledgment that Mr. de la Mare
and Mr. Eliot are writers of indubitable and
acknowledged talent. The thing which makes
our praise of contemporaries involuntarily too
high is the genuine desire that they should be
great, the necessity to see significance in our era,
whether it is precisely where we are discovering it
or not. Condemning a contemporary work a
critic can retain objectivity and measure, for he is
not seeing it through the magnifying glass of his
wishes; but as soon as he begins to praise, he is
carried away by his desires and his hopes, which
are far greater than the object he is considering,

and a modest virtue will make him believe that here is the fulfilment of all he has been unconsciously looking for. The illusions we have about contemporary literature are the measure of the power of the Zeit Geist, the Zeit Geist which can only continue to exist by appearing to justify itself in effectual expression, and which will finally convince us, therefore, that the expression is effectual.

The illusions of his period no writer has been able to throw off completely, for they are knit with the period's desires, and with what makes the artist create. If in Shakespeare there is not so much of the illusion of the Elizabethan age as in Marlowe, the inescapable residue remains. If Wordsworth and Shelley said fewer than Southey of the things which the mobilized forces of their environment made it inconceivable that they should not say, they said enough to show where mass suggestion ended and poetry began. When, giving voice to revolutionary ideas outworn, even pedantic, to us now, they announced the immediate dawn of a new era, they were not poets, but manifestations of their time; and it was only when, concerned with the further meaning of that

11

ideology, they tried to find something within themselves to justify it, that they attained utterance
true both to themselves and their era. In the
creative writer's struggle with the illusions of his
time there is a stage where the illusions become
truth, where, no longer influences or assumptions,
they are objectified as moments in the permanent experience of mankind. Yet it is the Zeit
Geist, the mass of suggestion, desire and suffering of the time, which differentiates one literary
period from another; by presenting a new resistance it provokes a new response.

To indicate the points at which a true resistance
has been faced in contemporary literature must be
infinitely difficult. Yet certain things are toler-
ably clear. The difference in quality between Mr.
Joyce's work and Mr. Huxley's is very suggestive.
Superficial resemblances there are many; both
writers are irreligious, both are disillusioned, both
are ironical; and the temper of the age is all three.
Yet the difference between Mr. Joyce's *quality* and
Mr. Huxley's is infinite. It may be indicated
broadly by saying that while Mr. Huxley's disillusionment is a thing which, with trifling varia-

tions, may be found among half the writers in
London and Paris, Mr. Joyce's may not. In
reading Mr. Huxley we may, if we choose, as-
sume his disillusionment, take it for granted as
comfortably as we take any habitual assumption.
But when disillusionment is objectified as it is in
Ulysses, we can no longer do this; we are compelled to reckon with it. We are not at liberty to
adopt it as it stands; for this disillusionment is no
longer an attitude, but rather all that an attitude
by its nature hides and keeps us from seeing. To
accept it is not thus to accept another disguise or
defence; it is rather to accept in some measure
ourselves. For its effect Mr. Huxley's work depends on the fact that we do tend to make the assumptions he makes; but once his mood is not
accepted as self-evident, his irony becomes empty;
we are left with a mere attitude, seductively presented, which has no grounds for existing save
that it is the attitude of a great number of people
who question it as little as Mr. Huxley does.
This is to say that Mr. Huxley's novels, in spite
of admirable qualities, a graceful style, wit, remarkable tact in avoiding the *bête,* belong to the

literature of fashion. A change of mood would take half their appositeness from them. *Ulysses,* on the other hand, depends very little for its comprehension on the mood which its readers take to it; for their floating disillusionment, half-conscious and vague, is there so profoundly grasped and completely objectified, that the general mood fades, evaporates, becomes unreal, beside it. We feel that this attitude has been radically modified, that henceforth it must become more real, or, if it persists, more unreal.

If Mr. Huxley is our best example of the fashionable writer, and Mr. Joyce of the artist expressing the age by an uncompromising opposition to it, there is another figure equally significant as a writer of escape. A great deal has been said against the literature of escape; but it is one of the types of literature, and will continue to be written so long as writers, like other men, adapt themselves in different ways to the world. Blake's poetry was in a sense a poetry of escape, and so was that of Wordsworth, Shelley, and Keats; and it would be pedantic to deny that it has enriched experience. For escape is one way

14

of saving oneself from being overwhelmed by the suggestion of the age, and of penetrating to a source of inspiration deeper than it. Mr. Lawrence is the grand example in our age of the poet of escape. He has scoured the globe to find some order of life sufficiently primitive to be the antithesis of contemporary Europe; and he has written violently against almost every modern form of thought and feeling. Yet in presenting in his novels such a radical antithesis to all the age stands for, he has brought a profound criticism to bear upon it. His values, his symbols, his hopes, are so opposed at every point to the spirit of the age that he makes us question not one or two, but all of its assumptions. The defect of the literature of escape is that it is too sweeping; it has neither the exactitude nor the practical temper of the literature of conflict. It postulates only two things: its vision of truth and beauty, and a world which does not correspond to that vision. Yet its criticism may be profound as far as it goes, for it apprehends the problem in its full and appalling form, though it can find no solution.

All the important writers of our time belong to

15

these two categories. In some there is a divided allegiance, in Mr. Eliot most strikingly, who in his poetry sets side by side the response of the poet who desires to escape from his environment, and that of the critic of life who wishes to come to terms with it. The rank of these writers will be determined by the thing which at present determines their value for us: the profundity, comprehensiveness and truth of their criticism of contemporary life.

JAMES JOYCE

⸺ II ⸺

JAMES JOYCE

I

No other novelist who has written in English has had a greater mastery than Mr. Joyce of language as an instrument of literary expression, and no one else, probably, has striven so consciously to attain it. *Dubliners* was an ideal apprentice piece for an artist; in it Mr. Joyce set himself to describe accurately the things he saw, attempting at the beginning what most writers achieve towards the end. The *Portrait of the Artist as a Young Man* marked a further stage. That book was as much a recreation of language as a record of experience. The marvellous dialogue which appeared first in it was not like the transcriptions of ordinary talk in *Dubliners;* it was a second language which was used consciously to vary and complete the lingual pattern of the work. That

19

pattern of speech seemed complete in itself, a thing of different nature from, but as real as, the events and experiences, many of them sordid, which it described. There were thus two values in the novel, separate, yet necessary to each other: the value of language and that of life, the value of art and that of experience. To Mr. Joyce the first of these is pure, the second mixed. Art must descend into life, the word must seek out all it can and enter into it; yet, having entered into it, it returns and remains pure in the consciousness of the artist. Life cannot soil it, but only a disobedience of its own laws.

In the *Portrait of the Artist as a Young Man* Mr. Joyce acquired the mastery of language, the knowledge of and reverence for its mysteries, which prepared him for *Ulysses*. He learnt, too, for the second time, the strict realism which, because it demands perfect exactitude in the rendering, is valuable as a discipline, makes an intensive demand on the artist's powers of expression, and by putting a strain on them enhances them. In embracing this realism he discarded the facile sensibility of his time, which was occupied

20

only with the secondary phenomena of consciousness—with the psychological effect of the object
rather than the object, with distinctions rather than
with things—and which in that preoccupation
while seizing the shadow lost the substance. The
Portrait of the Artist as a Young Man not only
left Mr. Joyce with a greater command over English than any other novelist had posssessed; it
was a sort of self-inoculation against a sensibility
grown burdensome. Without either of these
Ulysses could never have been written. For in
Ulysses the dual values of the *Portrait,* the values
of life and art, of reality and imagination, are
developed side by side until each attains its maximum of significance, and the discrepancy between them issues in a form of humour which
through its intellectual profoundity becomes universal. It is a humour not of fashion, nor of
character, but of the processes of life, those processes which create history and produce religions
and civilizations, while leaving the great part of
the human race, the average sensual man outside
us and within us, spiritually unchanged and apparently unchangeable. It sets forth the dreams

of religion, the magic of language, the splendours
of the intellect, the revolutions of history, over
against the simple facts: the naïvety of physical
desire, the functions of the body, the triviality of
the floating thoughts the body sends up into our
minds. A theme so tremendous could only be
expressed in great tragedy or great comedy, could
only in one of these two ways be lifted into a plane
where it no longer overwhelms us, and where having passed through it we are freed from its worst
oppression. Had Mr. Joyce not inoculated himself against sensibility by an overdose of realism
he could never have attained this emancipating
comic vision of the entire modern world. Had
he not been so sensitive that he suffered mon-
strously from his sensibility his comedy would
have had no driving power behind it. One feels
again and again in *Ulysses* that the uproarious-
ness of the farce, the recklessness of the blasphemy, is wildest where the suffering of the artist
has been most intense. A writer whose sufferings
were so great and so conscious needed a more
elaborate technique than most writers do, as much

to put a distance between himself and his sufferings as to express them.

Dubliners and the *Portrait* were a necessary preparation, an apprenticeship strengthening the artist against life. They were exercises working out a part of Mr. Joyce's problem; but in *Ulysses* the whole problem is faced and to the extent of Mr. Joyce's present powers resolved. That problem must needs have been the problem of all the things from which he suffered, for the sincere artist is distinguished from the rest by the fact that his essential concern is with the things which make him suffer, the things, in other words, which stand between him and freedom. There is thus a necessary and an organic relation between him and his work, to create being, as Ibsen said, an act of emancipation. But when, as in *Ulysses,* the creation is encyclopædic, when it attempts to gain freedom not from this or that, but from all the bonds, all the suffering, of the artist's soul, the impulse from which it started becomes a part of the autobiography of the book as well as of the writer. What Mr. Joyce suffered from in writ-

23

ing *Ulysses* was obviously in its completeness the life he had known; our modern world in all its intellectual manifestations as well as in its full banality; in its beliefs, its hopes, its charities, its reverences; its religion, patriotism, humanitarianism, science, literature, politics; its illusions as well as its realities. How could the full volume of all these burdensome hopes, theories, sensibilities, banalities, cruelties, meannesses, sensualities, be rendered in a work of art? Obviously not in a story, an action having a beginning, a development, a climax and an end, but rather in a record of the most obvious unit of time in which all these could manifest themselves, in that unit of time which begins with something recalling birth and ends in something resembling death: in a day. *Ulysses* is a complete course, a set banquet, of the modern consciousness. And being that no other unit could have served; the author could not have got into the record of a year what he has got into the record of a day.

But this banquet of the modern consciousness was to be a comic summing up as well as a banquet; it was to be not only abundant, but so bur-

densomely, absurdly abundant that all the courses
would be made to appear ridiculous, as Rabelais
made the courses of the medieval banquet ridiculous. And as Mr. Joyce's encyclopædic plan
justified the time unit of his chronicle, so his comic
intention justified the minuteness of his portrayal,
his huge accumulation of imaginative material.
His humour is on one side, like that of Rabelais,
a piling up of one burden on the mind after another until the breaking point is reached—the
breaking point of laughter. It operates by op-
pressing us consciously with all the things which
oppress us unconsciously, and by exaggerating
all this until it seems ridiculous that we should
bear it, or more exactly that it should exist at all.
A sense of this or that anomaly in social relations,
the sense which finds expression in polite comedy,
is far too light to shift this immense weight. To
do that comedy must include as many factors as
the greatest tragedy; it must embrace not only
man, but all that he believes in, the whole anthropomorphic cosmos. But even when the absurdities of the spirit are piled up in this way
they are still not in the realm of universal comedy:

the last touch is still wanting. That is given by
a running contrast between the vast symbols invented by man and his simple earthly reactions,
between the extravagance of belief and the simplicity of fact, the decency of civilized life and
the unseemliness of instinct. That was the mainspring of Rabelais' humour, and it is also that of
Mr. Joyce's. The more absurd and minute the
description of physiological reactions, the greater
obviously the effect. On the one hand an infinite immensity, on the other an infinitesimal
smallness; the intellectual dreams and spiritual
struggles of Stephen Dedalus in the one balance,
the vagaries of Leopold Bloom's instincts in the
other; around us the phantoms our minds have
created, and within us the utilitarian functions of
our bodies. And as the intellectual shapes which
man has conceived to be first a release and then
a burden are exaggerated, so his physical idiosyncrasies, his trifling thoughts, are refined upon.
There is in Mr. Joyce's obscenity as in that of
Rabelais an intellectual quality, as if in searching
the recondite secrets of the natural processes of the
body he were trying to penetrate to an unconscious

humour of the cells, of those elementary principles of life which have built up not only the body but all this phantasmal structure which we call thought, religion and civilization. His emphasis on the unseemly, on what, in other words, we have surpassed, depend upon, and wish to forget, is, at any rate, a necessary element in this kind of humour and an essential part of the plan of *Ulysses*. It is perverse, that is to say, intellectualized deliberately, but so it had to be to achieve its purpose.

The vision of the world whose mainspring is in this radical sense of contrast is one which, if it did not issue in humour, would be nightmare. In *Ulysses* it does not always issue in humour. The brothel scene is horrible partly because it is a misshapen birth, because, conceived as a grand example of the humour of horror, it attains through its failure an atmosphere of horror which because it is unintentional is strictly monstrous, and incapable of being resolved either into art or into human experience. This scene is a work of genius; it is more astonishing than anything else Mr. Joyce has written; but it has the portentous appearance of something torn from the womb of imagination, not the completeness of something born of it. We derive from it a vivid notion of the monstrous suffering through which the artist is passing; but here he has not passed beyond it; and we suffer equally as participators in the horrors of a raw experience and as spectators of a heroic but unavailing attempt to escape from it and set it in the realm of freedom. Had Mr. Joyce succeeded with this gigantic scene he would have produced something supreme in literature and not merely something supremely astounding and terrifying. It was obviously designed to be the climax of the work; in it the last resources of the theme were to be brought on the stage; the unconscious desires which up to now had been allowed only a chance or oblique expression were to come nakedly to the surface and attain freedom. They do not attain freedom. The brothel scene is not a release of all the oppressions and inhibitions of life in our time; it is rather a gigantic attempt to attain release.

But if we grant this crucial failure in the book, and a number of minor failures, there remains

more comedy in the grand style than has appeared
in our literature since the Elizabethan age. The
last chapter has been much praised, but there are
others only less admirable. The scene in the
pub. where Bloom is routed by the Citizen produces by an openly mechanical technique Mr.
Joyce's sense of contrast between an ordinary
happening in all its banality and richness and
the fantastic and etiolated symbols which the desires of men and the conventions of literature discover for it. Here it is the obviousness of the
means, the mechanical ease with which the simple
event assumes conventional or lofty forms in the
fancy, that is at the root of the humour. We
seem to see the illusions at their normal work.
The banal fact and the fantastic interpretation
are both present before our eyes, are both obvious
and credible (the one arising spontaneously from
the other), and are both ridiculous. The chapter of parodies, which has been so much criticized,
is still more remarkable. There we see the figure
of Mr. Bloom passing, as it were, through a
comic pageant of the English spirit. In his
progression he assumes a sort of absurd uni-

versality; he is a man "of Israel's folk . . . that on earth wandering far had fared"; he is "childe Leopold" and "sir Leopold that had for his cognizance the flower of quiet," and "Master Calmer," and "Leop. Bloom of Crawford's journal sitting snug with a covey of wags," and "Mr. L. Bloom (Pubb. Canv.)." He is a type, and a succession of types through history, and a multiplication of types in space; one person in himself and many persons in time and in the minds of men. In this scene Mr. Joyce's comic imagination is at its height; it raises Mr. Bloom into a legendary figure and gives him history and the world for his stage. But in doing that it fulfils once more the requirements of Mr. Joyce's humour, for to squat Mr. Bloom on the centre of that stage was to attain a comic vision of the world and of history.

What is it that through this use of contrast, this breaking of our resistances by accumulation, Mr. Joyce tries to set in the plane of low comedy? First of all, professional seriousness of all kinds, and secondly the objects about which people are serious in this way: religion, to which the comic reaction is blasphemy; patriotism, to which it is little less; literature, to which it is parody; the claims of science, to which it is an application of anti-climax; sex, to which it is obscenity. When comedy attempts to become universal it has perforce to include blasphemy and obscenity, for these are the two poles of this comedy just as the soul and the body are the two poles of human existence. To see religion with the eyes of comedy is not, of course, to laugh it out of existence, any more than to see sex comically is to destroy it. All that comedy can destroy is strictly the second-rate, everything that is not in its mode the best, everything less genuine than the genuine —a class of thoughts and emotions which make up the preponderating part of the experience of most people and of all ages, and is a permanent burden which at times may become unbearable. Books such as *Ulysses* and *Gargantua* can only be written out of an almost insupportable feeling of oppression; for humour on this scale the sense of oppression is needed as a driving power. The load of oppression which Rabelais cleared away we can recognize now clearly enough; it is more difficult to realize, although it is easy to feel, what

31

it is that oppresses in our age a creative writer
like Mr. Joyce.   But when the reverences of any
time are taken very seriously and not very intensely, when a belief in enlightenment, progress
and humanity becomes habitual, and men act and
think with a fearful eye on it and on the most
mediocre of its priests, it has already become as
injurious to the creative impulse as the strictest
obscurantism could be.   It is a weight of second-
rate sentiment and thought, and the time comes
when the only thing to be done is to clear it away.

To destroy so completely as Mr. Joyce does in
Ulysses is to make a new start.   Or more exactly,
the new start must have been made before the
destruction began, for the new thing destroys only
that it may have room to grow in freedom.   But
what is new in this sense in *Ulysses* it is hazardous
to attempt to say yet; for the things which are
most new in it have a breath of an antiquity which
seems to antedate the antiquity of classical literature, and to come out of a folk rather than a
literary inspiration.   Mr. Joyce's prostitutes in
the brothel scene exist neither in the world of
literature, as that world has been conceived almost

since its beginning, nor in the world of fact.
They are rather figures in a folk-lore which mankind continually creates, or rather carries with it;
creations and types in the dream in which sensual humanity lives, and which to humanity is
the visible world. This folk-lore, which is the
æsthetic utterance of the illiterate classes and of
the illiterate parts of our nature, which co-exists
with literature, but in a separate world—is not
inarticulate; but it expresses itself anonymously,
and is such a constant attribute of human life that
it rarely feels the need of the more permanent, the
more specialized, expression of art. It attains its
perfection from day to day by means which are as
suited to its purposes as the means of literature
are to the purposes of literature. Yet from it
literature arose, for like literature, it is æsthetic,
and has the freedom of perception which can only
come when men are delivered from their utilitarian
prejudices. And to it accordingly literature must
periodically come back, as much to test as to
renew itself. This is the world to which Mr.
Joyce has in part returned, in part striven to return, in *Ulysses*. He has seen, as only a pro-

found theorist on art could have seen, that the
sources of art lie here, and that here is the primary
division in our consciousness from which flow on
the one hand the laws of art, and on the other
the laws of the practical world in which we live.
The great categories of literature, such as the
pathetic, the tragic, and the comic, which with
the interior development of literature tend ever to
become more pure, more formal, Mr. Joyce has
related to the loose and undifferentiated categories
of popular imagination, and, starting from these,
has set out to attain a more essential pathos, a
more complete comedy, than the conventions of
modern literature could have given him. He has
not escaped the dangers of such an ambitious attempt. In *Ulysses* there are passages of unas-
similated folk-lore which we feel do not belong to
literature—diurnal phrases of Dublin talk which
should not have survived the day, which, perfect
in their time and place, get a false emphasis when
set deliberately into the frame of a work of imagination. But where the attempt is successful,
Mr. Joyce's imagination has a unique immediacy,
a unique originality. In one glance we seem to

see the life which he describes immediately before and immediately after he has set his seal upon it, and the transformation of reality into art takes place, as it were, under our eyes. Then we feel sometimes that in sweeping aside the æsthetic sense of three centuries, Mr. Joyce has penetrated to the æsthetic consciousness in itself, the æsthetic consciousness, that is to say, before it has become selective and exclusive, as the more it is developed and refined it tends to become. It is, of course, obvious that the totality of the responses of that consciousness cannot be rendered in literature, of which selection is not merely a virtue, but also the condition. Yet in the history of literature, as has often been shown, the principle of selection sometimes becomes a conventional, an arbitrary one, and, indeed, continually tends to do so; and, therefore, it is at rare times necessary for the artist to put himself in a position where a fundamental act of selection becomes compulsory, and where he feels that every decision, whether to include or to reject, is significant not only on traditional grounds, but is made by his own unconditional volition and as if for the first time. *Ulysses* not only raises the problem of selection again; in part, it answers it by bringing into literature things banished from it, as we now see more clearly, on moral and conventional rather than essential grounds. In doing that, Mr. Joyce has both enriched literature and potentially widened its scope.

II

Ulysses showed the direction in which literature for ten years had been moving; it showed also the direction, or rather some of the directions, in which—who knows for how long?—it will move. Into it various currents, Irish, cosmopolitan, personal, came together, and out of it they issued again clarified and transformed. Analyzing *Ulysses* one might have drawn a chart of the future of literature, showing not only what would be attempted, but also what with good luck would be achieved; or rather one might have done so if among the various streams collected together in *Ulysses* there had not been one, and the most potent, which, mingling with the others, changed them, contributed to them something occult.

36

This was Mr. Joyce's genius, over which nobody but himself had control. For the rest he not only hammered out a new grammar of literary art in *Ulysses;* he discovered a new field of æsthetic experience (a field on which others had laboured without knowing what it was); and to describe it he invented a magic of speech unessayed for a long time. It was because he went back so far to the fundamentals of art that his book had its enigmatic, primal atmosphere, and seemed, in spite of its modernity, hoary with years. One did not know whether to be astonished most by Mr. Joyce's systematic method or his discoveries, by his discoveries or his inventions. He renewed both the subject-matter of literature and the speech in which artists may for some time express it. He found the language for which Mr. George Moore made an unsuccessful voyage to Dublin, but which was there, and in other parts of the world, all the time. He evoked in certain collocations of words a malignant necromancy such as poets have found in certain landscapes, calling out their hidden evil. That his magic was always black magic was the chief sign of his limitation as

an artist.   He was concerned with the roots of life
and not with its flowering; and where life has
not yet blossomed, where the unconscious has not
yet freed and attenuated itself in the conscious
(as for example in the lives of primitive peoples,
in our dreams, in our blind desires), all magic is
black magic.   Mr. Joyce went over the conscious
life of men like a plough and showed the richness
of the soil; and *Ulysses* gives us the sense of
black magic which ploughed fields sometimes
evoke.   This feeling is probably a racial memory
of times which saw the birth of magic, when the
blackness of the upturned earth was an image to
men of blasphemous violation and of inexplicable
increase.

But everything in *Ulysses* has this mythical
quality, and the humour is, like that of primitive
peoples, the humour of size.   Whatever validity
there may be philosophically in Mr. Joyce's symbolical construction, in which each part of the
book represents an organ of the human body, and
the whole the human form divine, its humorous
virtues are so clear that they leap out and strike
the eye.   Mr. Bloom is conceived on such an ex-

travagant scale that he gives the effect of one of those Brobdingnagians who to Gulliver must have had the appearance of a landscape with spreading plains, rising peaks, thick woods and flowing streams. Now and then a single feature springs into grotesque prominence; we regard a nose as big as the side of a mountain, we climb over it, survey it, measure it; we see cheeks swelling like hills, eyes gleaming like lakes. To regard things in this way was a secret of primitive humour, and it found expression in the preoccupation of early man with giants and with the vast creatures which we call dragons; for these had an aspect comical as well as dreadful. It is the method which Mr. Joyce practises on Leopold Bloom, going back here to the sources of æsthetic emotion. Mr. Bloom is one of the great comic figures in literature. He is humorous not only in the tricks of his temperament and his mind, but like Falstaff in those of his body; and it is an artistic heresy to hold that the body is unworthy the regard of the spirit, and that Falstaff's belly had any less right to æsthetic expression than the lids of Juno's eyes. As a comic figure Mr. Bloom is so

completely, so magnificently shown, that in regarding him we seem to be watching at its play
the humour of the processes of life. Mr. Joyce
has pursued comedy down to its source, penetrating to the cells, to the dust out of which man rises.
Through its minuteness his humour becomes universal, and gives one the feeling that not only men
might feel warmed by it, but all the forms of that
nature in which copulation and reproduction are
omnipotent. It is a humour entirely of the
earth, as perhaps all humour is.

It is a humour, too, in which extravagance is
reinstated after being banished for a long time as
childish and contrary to mature taste. In primitive humour there is something outrageous, and
the humorist not only discloses the foibles and
indecencies of his audience but flaunts his own,
piling them up in a mountain and squatting upon
it. This humour was an intellectual parody of
the saturnalia, a little more wild in its imaginary
excesses than the original. It was a great emotional and intellectual release, and it carried with
it a total abnegation of dignity. Later came the
comic artist who in making his audience laugh

retained a sober countenance, admitting no fellow-
ship with the frailties and lusts which in describing he satirized or excused. This has been the
fashion of the last three centuries, a polite fashion
in which the original flavour of humour was refined away. Comedy in this style amused men
and made them resigned to their lot, thus fulfilling
both a social and an ethical purpose; but it no
longer gave them release. It was something different from humour in its first rude state, its
means restraint and economy where originally they
had been extravagance and grotesque abundance.
Disregarding the fashion of centuries Mr. Joyce
has recaptured the boundlessness of primitive
humour. He has not been ashamed to play the
clown, to resurrect the mock-heroic, which everybody thought was safely buried, and to practise
parody, which nobody considered a form worth
the notice of an artist of serious purpose. And
to all these he has given new significance, prov-
ing their possibilities. The part of *Ulysses* where
the thoughts of Gerty MacDowell are presented in
the manner of a penny novelette is not only
parody; it is a unique and poignant form of ex-

pression, a doubly indirect, a multiple utterance, in which almost everything is left to be implied, and the triteness of the words conceals half-a-dozen meanings, some of them of an ethereal beauty. In handling subject-matter so trivial and so hackneyed as this Mr. Joyce shows most clearly the originality of his mind and the incisiveness of his art. His parodies of the daily newspapers do not merely amuse; they evoke a gigantic image of the fatuity of the mind. Things which we accept with an ineradicable laziness as modes he portrays as aspects of a profound folly, a still more profound stupidity; and, recognizing that it is not the press but the human intellect that he is parodying, we are not merely diverted, we are edified. He uses parody as a means of anatomizing the mind, showing that it, too, has its absurdities, its gigantic humours, as unavoidable, in spite of its dignity, as of those of the body; and by an extravagance calculated in its seeming excess he reaches the essential in a new way.

But as if these things were not enough he has described clearly for the first time the realm only half-glimpsed by writers such as Mr. D. H. Lawrence, Mr. Sherwood Anderson and Miss Dorothy Richardson. He has revealed the swarming world of sub-conscious and half-conscious thoughts which constitute three-fourths of our life, and he has shown that it has a magical and excessive beauty. In hardly any other work of modern times is there such an overpowering sense of the inexhaustibility of human life. That he has succeeded in articulating a new world in a new language one cannot say; one feels that here and there he has won only an approximate success; but that he has achieved so much is astonishing. He has made at least a rough anatomy of the dark god whom Mr. Lawrence sees only in glimpses and mentions only in hints; and if the outline is cloudy it is chiefly because the lineaments are huge. In *Ulysses* the total articulation of the sub-conscious body of man is obscured by the separate features; but by study if not by intuition they can be put together. The separate merits of the book we can apprehend immediately as we apprehend anything that in art is beautiful, but to appreciate its total beauty we have to draw upon reflection.

43

This fault *Ulysses* has; it has another which is more serious. For such a huge and multifarious work it is too continuously in one key. Rabelais, whom Mr. Joyce recalls constantly, wrote encyclopædically and minutely of the physical part of man, but he wrote also of man's spiritual part, giving it, too, its due tribute; and this is what makes Rabelais so satisfying. Mr. Joyce is encyclopædic; he is learnedly minute; but he is not satisfying, simply because one part of life he almost completely ignores; and by its lack of relief *Ulysses* sometimes oppresses us: the complementary part of our nature is interdicted expression. Mr. Joyce's book has neither the breadth nor the sanity of supreme comic art; its richness is not quite that of nature: the atmosphere is overheated, and the horizon is too narrow for the objects which are crowded into it. In *Ulysses* life presses in too closely upon us on every side; too closely for us to see it clearly. That is as much as to say that Mr. Joyce has not won a complete triumph over his subject-matter.

But his attempt is great, and his measure of success, considering the magnitude of the task, re-

44

markable. No imaginative work of our time has so much of the unpredictable quality of genius. In *Ulysses* the author has brought literary art back to its sources, and he has remained at them, drawing continuously from the fountainhead. The book has the quality which the Germans call *ursprunglich;* it is not a new mode of art, but rather a fundamental assertion of it. Consequently no work of our time has so completely the atmosphere and the authority of a scripture. It is the full utterance, enigmatic but not to be ignored, of one man. And like all scriptures it contains within it a principle of differentiation; many streams lead out from it, and it may well become the central point of a literature. The danger is not that it will remain unrecognized, but that in time it will overshadow some of the other potentialities of our age. Yet, though it may fetter the talents of a few artists, to many it will give their opportunity. On every side it is a beginning, and a beginning is what our generation has chiefly desired.

45

D. H. LAWRENCE

～ III ～

D. H. LAWRENCE

MR. LAWRENCE's most obviously striking quality
as a writer is a kind of splendour, not of the spirit,
nor of the mind, but of the senses and the instincts.
His spirit is exalted only when it takes fire from
his senses; his mind follows the fluctuations of
his desires, intellectualizing them, not operating
in its own right.   But his senses can be set alight
by anything natural.   They reach far, downwards
and upwards, and they drink joy from everything
they touch.   The sun and moon, the sea, trees
and flowers, animals, sex, instinctive love and
hatred—of all these he has written in a new way,
and as if he were not their observer, but a mystical sharer in their being.   They absorb him into
themselves while he writes, but, having absorbed
him, they give him their riches, suffusing his
senses, and through them his mind and soul, with

a confused magic which is purely of the earth.
So it is often difficult in reading him to tell
whether his magic is a satisfaction of his being
or a bondage, whether he is exercising it or is in
its power. His novels produce always a double
impression—of a breaking through, and of an
imprisonment in the strange and beautiful, but
subterranean, realm to which he has broken
through. From this subterranean place he sees a
far richer world than others do who are content
with the light of day. His trees and flowers he
sees, as it were, from the inside; they have an interior glow and a violence of being which could
only be rendered by one who by an unconditional
act of imagination entered into their life. Mr.
Lawrence's imagination has done this so completely that it has never entirely emerged again.
There seems nothing which it cannot enter into,
either in nature or in the instinctive life of men
and women. It recoils solely before most of the
things in which the imagination has till now found
its inspiration: the conscious life of mankind,
ordinary relations and problems, the tragedy and
comedy of life as we know it. Mr. Lawrence has

deepened these for us, but he has also dived beneath them so far that in effect he ignores them.
And that is because he is on the side of the instincts, and against all the forms, emasculated or
deformed, in which they can be manifested in a
civilized society. His view of life is one-sided
in a magnificent and obvious way, like the instincts, or like nature.

This one-sidedness, however, is the chief source
of his strength as well as of his weakness. It is
his identification of himself with nature which
gives him that extraordinary knowledge of natural
potencies which seems occult to more rational
minds. The identification is so close that in
describing nature he writes not merely like one
who sees with his eyes and his imagination, but
like one whose whole being, whose blood, lusts,
instincts, and senses are ecstatically sharing in
the life of the thing described. We smell and
touch the objects he describes, and he makes us
feel such things as heat and cold, growth and de-
cay, more vividly than any other writer. His
landscapes are vivid not because they are visually
clear, but because they are intensely apprehended

by all the senses together, as if there were between Mr. Lawrence and nature an unspoken masonic understanding. They are peculiarly radiant and full, yet dreamlike, as if they were reflected not in the mind but in the blood.

Even his most rapid descriptions have this dreamlike quality. When in *The Boy in the Bush* Jack Grant rides after the kangaroo, we do not see the grey scrub, the grey-white sand, the yellow light, as vividly as Mr. Masefield would have made us see them, and Mr. Forster would have given us a clearer impression of movement and flying trees. With Mr. Lawrence, on the other hand, we pass through a very vivid but rather vague experience, in which we seem to see something in Jack Grant passing into the landscape, and something in the landscape passing into him. This out- and in-flowing communicates to everything a heightened life; the substance of experience is changed as if by alchemy. A communication has been established, a number of potencies have been released; and these alter everything. The horses which follow Ursula Brangwen over the wet field in *The Rainbow* give

us the same feeling. They are not visual entities merely, nor are they psychological ideas in
Ursula's mind. They are rather instincts which
have suddenly become articulate, and which communicate with Ursula through the unconscious
language of identification and repulsion—the two
great forces which in their many forms Mr. Lawrence has described again and again in his novels
and poems. For this unconscious communication all his characters strive; it is their fulfilment,
and the intellect has hardly any part in it. On
this field everything in his novels happens. He
has not deliberately sought it out for description.
On the contrary, it is plainly the realm of consciousness which he can best describe.

Nature he comprehends mainly through identification: mankind he comprehends almost as
much through repulsion. What he understands
in his characters is not the qualities which make
up their personalities, but rather the thing which
arouses this unconscious attraction or repulsion:
their natural foundation, healthy or the reverse.
He apprehends this exactly and subtly, with an
unconscious knowledge which men in cultivating

their intellects have almost lost, and the remaining remnants of which they distrust. But Mr. Lawrence trusts this unconscious knowledge more than anything else. The responses of his instincts are not merely phenomena to him, to be judged by the mind; they are truths whose force is conclusive. What he tells us about his characters is simply what these responses tell him.

It is difficult to define what that is. But if we were to grant that the instinctive body of man had an outline of its own, forming a large and fluctuating envelope surrounding his actual body, then that would be what Mr. Lawrence habitually describes. Action arises in his novels when the instinctive field of one character impinges on that of another, producing something like an electric shock. Two vital principles are enraged, violated, or glorified by each other, while the mind looks on and knows its irrelevance. Thus Fate in Mr. Lawrence's novels is not woven by character, but by instincts which colour character, and sometimes seem independent of it. He has described these as they have never been described before. He shows them in all their states: in

their insatiability, their almost mystical peace
when they are at rest, their cunning which makes
them move crookedly to their goal, their acrid
surrender when they are finally defeated, their
wisdom which is like that of a being of vast experience.

His problem as an artist was to present clearly
this drama of the instincts. In reckoning up his
success and failure one must take account not
only of his achievement, but of the difficulties of
his task. These were enormous. He had to
translate into a conscious thing, language, states
which are fluid and unconscious, and cannot be
directly denoted.

He tried to do this by employing a peculiarly
telepathic style, a style which does not render
things so much as the feeling of things. Sometimes merely an unavailing struggle with language, a senselessly repeated assault which does
not break through, this style has splendid moments when it sets the object before us in the full
glow of its aura. His dialogue is a graph of the
movements of the instincts: it does not depict
character, nor define situation. Like his nar-

rative style, it has an underlying content, suggested by the words, but not contained in them.

So his characters sometimes say things which as conscious statement are absurd, while as delineation of the unconscious they are true. In *The Rainbow*, for example, Skrebensky's "heart grew smaller, it began to fuse like a bead. He knew he would die." But he does not die, he is not even at a supreme crisis in his life; Mr. Lawrence takes him through many more crises of the same kind. Again, in *The Boy in the Bush*, Jack Grant "could feel his body, the English cool body of his being, slowly melting down and being invaded by a new tropical quality. Sometimes he said to himself, he was sweating his soul away. That was how it felt: as if he were sweating his soul away. And he let his soul go, let it melt away out of his wet hot body." Yet in the next chapter there is no sign of this tremendous change. Things like these happen constantly in Mr. Lawrence's novels, and that is bad; it shows that he has not found the indisputable form for his thought. But there is a justification in imagination for them; they are true to the workings of instincts. For the instincts are only concerned, so far as we know, with absolutes. They recognize only things like life and its opposite. For a frustration or an insurmountable obstacle they have only a word like "death." And so, in delineating the instincts, it was a fine stroke of imagination to omit the conditional, which only belongs to conscious life, and to set absolute against absolute, life against death, stating both opposites in their full power, and indicating in the fluctuating line through which they flow into each other the line of life. The outline which emerges is not that of life as we know it, but it is something which deeply corresponds to it.

Mr. Lawrence, then, secures his effect thus far, though in a manner which commits him to an almost habitual exaggeration. He shows us the life of the instincts. But he has never shown us an instinct coloured by the personality which it occupies: he has never drawn a complete character. We remember the scenes in his novels; we forget the names of his men and women. We should not know any of them if we were to meet them in the street, as we should know Anna Karenina, or Crevel, or even Soames Forsyte. We never ask ourselves whether they would have done this or that; we have never met people like them, or rather everybody we have met is, at a certain unpredictable level, like them. They are not men and women; they are male and female. They all love in the same way, or at most in two or three ways. Any of them may become one of the others at one of those crises in Mr. Lawrence's novels when everything is dissolved in instinct. Jack Grant is the good, natural man in *The Boy in the Bush,* Easu, the bad; yet Jack is often given Easu's emotions, and becomes Easu when he is directly opposed to him, reaching identification through hatred.

Thus character in Mr. Lawrence's novels is always melting into instinct, and human nature into nature pure and simple. He does outline a struggle, vague and obsessed, between the humanly acquired attributes of his characters and instinct, but that struggle would be infinitely more moving if the two sides were more equally balanced. He was right in making the struggle vague, for it is vague; it has not the clarity which

moralists and theologians have given it. But he
was wrong in not stating more impressively the
second, the conscious, factor, as essential as the
first. In that he shows most clearly his chief
limitation: his necessity to be always on one side,
and to realize it so intensely that he becomes blind
to the other. So he is unfair to everything conscious—to civilization, the mind, character, in all
of which art finds so much of its subject-matter.
He has written about these in his essays, but he
has never brought them into his art. He desires,
one sometimes feels, to build up again on the basis
of the instincts all that has already been built up,
partly on them and partly on other things. He
hates the intellect when it is free and working by
its own laws, for he wishes it to be an extension,
perhaps a sublimation, of the instincts, and to say
over again in a different language what they say.
So he has little appreciation of the mind, the soul
and character, in themselves. He shows us one
marvellous province of life, but not, like the great
artists, life itself.

The tragedy in his novels is a tragedy not of
outward misfortune, nor of personality, but rather

59

of subterranean defeat. The agonized breaking of an instinct against an obstacle too strong for it is a recurring motive in his novels. In *England, My England* the young wife "prayed beside the bed of her child. And like the Mother with the seven swords in her breast, slowly her heart of pride and passion died in her breast, bleeding away. Slowly it died, bleeding away, and she turned to the Church for comfort, to Jesus, to the Mother of God, but most of all to that great and enduring institution, the Roman Catholic Church. She withdrew into the shadow of the Church. She was a mother with three children. But in her soul she died, her heart of pride and passion and desire bled to death, her soul belonged to the Church, her body belonged to her duties as a mother." It is clear that this kind of tragedy is not fully human, for the simple reason that when the unconscious powers of the character are exhausted, there is no conscious power left to carry on the struggle. The will is not merely weak and inarticulate, it is in abeyance; it does not come into action. To this tremendous extent the tragedy in Mr. Lawrence's novels fails in significance. It is a tragedy almost purely of nature rather than of human nature; it might befall a lion caged or a tree mutilated as easily as a human being thwarted in his unconscious desires. It is new in literature, it is sometimes very beautiful, but it has not the full significance of human tragedy.

The revolt against the forms of conscious life was in Mr. Lawrence's work at the beginning. It was only formulated intellectually in his later works. But the formulation did not mark a true development; it did not enrich and clarify his art, but made it didactic. His vision is not more lucid now than it was in *The Rainbow;* his philosophy is only more set and clear. That philosophy, in other words, has not been fused with his art; it has been arbitrarily imposed upon it. So we have a novel like *Kangaroo,* which is mostly loose discussion, and a tale like *The Captain's Doll,* which is falsified to point a moral. More and more Mr. Lawrence's theories are encroaching on his art, and pushing it out. And this misfortune was bound to happen, simply because his art has never attained clarity in itself, and therefore something possessing clarity had to be set alongside it to illumine it. Through an inner weakness, or that negligence which he dignifies into arrogance, Mr. Lawrence has not brought his art to its perfection; and he theorizes because there is something which he cannot see clearly enough to describe.

There remain his gifts, splendid in their imperfection, thrown recklessly into a dozen books, fulfilling themselves in none. His chief title to greatness is that he has brought a new mode of seeing into contemporary literature, a new beauty which is also one of the oldest things in the world. It is the beauty of the ancient instinctive life which civilized man has almost forgotten. Mr. Lawrence has picked up a thread of life left behind by mankind, and at some time it will be woven in with the others, making human life more complete, as all art tends to do. He has written of what he has rediscovered as only a great writer could. Life has come to him fresh from the minting at a time when it seemed to everyone either soiled or banal. He has many faults, and several of these are wilful. He has not fulfilled the promise shown in *Sons and Lovers* and *The Rain-bow*.   He has not submitted himself to any discipline.   But if he has not written any completely satisfying work, he has written in almost all his books more greatly than any other English writer of his time.

VIRGINIA WOOLF

~IV~

VIRGINIA WOOLF

THE historian writing fifty years hence of the literature of to-day will find in it a certain note of inhumanity. He will speak of our hostility to mankind, and he will remark how different Mr. James Joyce's attitude to his characters is from that of Scott, for example, or Jane Austen. A thorough dislike of their creations characterizes, indeed, the majority of modern novelists. Mr. Joyce hates and scorns his characters; Mr. Huxley's inspire him with disgust or with ill-natured laughter; Mr. Lawrence hews his down right and left in the name of his "dark god"; Mr. Stephen Hudson submits his, most severe test of all, to a scrupulous intellectual scrutiny. These writers do not accept the character as an end in himself; he is always a means to them; he is always on a different plane from the mind which evoked him.

67

The contemporary novelist does not walk through his crowds, on easy terms with them, good and bad, as Fielding and Thackeray walked through theirs. He is not among the works of his hands, but detached from them; he watches their movements as a scientist might watch the progress of an experiment. Jane Austen, we feel, is always at the excursions and tea parties she describes; she is one of the characters, the least observed and most observant of all. But this can scarcely be said of Mr. Joyce, or Mr. Huxley, or Mr. Hudson, even when they are portraying figures clearly autobiographical. There is always detachment in their spirit, a certain hostile watchfulness, a barrier of conscious or unconscious irony. They do not meet their characters on the same level as we should, if we were given the chance.

It may be said of Mrs. Woolf that she does meet her characters on this level. She accepts them as ends; she accepts them, that is to say, as people of the same status and existing in the same dimension as herself. She might walk into her novels and be at home in them. She stands in the same relation to her characters as almost all the chief

68

English novelists have stood to theirs. Her attitude, like theirs, is eminently practical, tolerant, appreciative, intelligent; it has the good sense and sagacity of the English prose tradition.

The point is important, for an easy coming and going between the mind of the novelist and the world he creates has characterized the bulk of great fiction. It characterizes all the Russian fiction we know; it characterizes French fiction to the time of Flaubert; it has characterized English fiction up to Mr. Joyce and Mr. Lawrence. The advantage it gives to the novelist is clear. It endows his imaginary world with an everyday actuality, a toughness which will stand wear and tear. It insensibly inclines us to the useful illusion that all we are reading about is actual; and when we once believe that, the background of the world will fill in readily behind it, as it fills in behind the happenings we hear of in actual life. But for the artist himself the pragmatic attitude has deeper virtues. If it does not make his imagination more profound, it makes it, at any rate, more dependable, sets it working more thoroughly. His relation to his characters being horizontal, being, that is to say, on the same plane if in one important respect not the same, as the relations of the characters among themselves, he will understand their reactions to each other more naturally and feel them more concretely than he could if he were surveying them from a height, if he were sinking his mind into them instead of sharing it with them. For this practical, everyday, distinctively prose way of approaching the theme perhaps the best term is intelligence. It is not a purely intellectual quality; it consists rather in the use of the intellect and the imagination in a comprehensive but commonsense way, as if, exercised on imaginary situations, they were being exercised on the actual problems of life.

The quality of intelligence Mrs. Woolf has in a high degree. It is to be seen equally and is of the same quality in her novels and in her volume of essays, *The Common Reader*; for intelligence works by the same means, whatever theme may confront it. All the notable English novelists of the past have possessed it; the only contemporary novelist, besides Mrs. Woolf, who has it in a striking degree is Mr. E. M. Forster. Mr. Joyce lacks it completely. He has a powerful, erratic intellect, but it is the differentiated intellect of the artist; it is hardly concerned at all with what is normal, expedient, practicable, but simply with what is, whether it should be humanly possible or impossible. Mr. Joyce has objectified magnificently his personal world, but it is not a world in which we could live, and to him that is, indeed, a matter of no concern. Yet it is a matter of the first importance in the actual world, and an imaginative work which ignores it ignores something essential; that work may have truth, but it will not be an approximate image of the truth. Mrs. Woolf's novels are an approximate image of the truth. The world she shows us is not of such vast dimensions as Mr. Joyce's, but it is on a perfect scale: there are all the elements in it that there are in any of the worlds we actually live in, and there is, moreover, a perpetual reference to the world itself, the modern world which looms behind and makes possible our smaller, personal worlds.

Width and justice of comprehension are chiefly necessary in the writer who tries to grasp all these implications and strives to make the picture complete. They were shown in Mrs. Woolf's first novel, *The Voyage Out;* they were shown still more remarkably in *Night and Day.* Nothing was more striking in these first two books than the undeviating sobriety of treatment, the absence of facility, the resolve to take all the factors into account and to be just to them all. The convention of the novel is accepted. The author, we feel, has resolved to take the novel as it is, and to make it do all that up to now it has done. In *The Voyage Out* she uses among other methods that of Chekhov. That book is still a little tentative, but *Night and Day,* which followed it, remains in some ways the finest of Mrs. Woolf's novels. In depth, in meaning behind meaning, some of the scenes in it are superior to anything else written in our time. The meeting between Denham and Rodney on the Embankment, the description of Katherine's aimless wanderings through London on the evening that she broke her appointment with Denham, the Hilbery household, the delightful but pathetic irrelevancies of Mrs. Hilbery: these, brought intimately together

in the book as they would be in life, give us the
sense of the rich variety of existence which only
Mrs. Woolf's predecessors in the English novel
can give. Certain complex effects which were
once characteristic of the English novel, effects in
which comedy and tragedy jostle, have been almost entirely lost in our time. Sterne was perhaps the first great prose master of them; Scott is
full of them; by Dickens they are exploited freely
but crudely. The conversation between Bartoline
Saddletree and Davie Deans about the trial of
Effie is a perfect example of this style; but we find
it again and again in Scott; it is an element in
almost all his great scenes. Nothing perhaps can
give us a stronger sense of the reality of the situation we are reading about than this juxtaposition
of the comic and the tragic. We feel that the
writer has seen all its aspects, even the most unexpected, that his imagination has not been canal-
ized by the theme, but is free and can move as it
wills. Intelligence once more, the taking of all
the factors into account, produces these imaginative juxtapositions; and in *Night and Day* it
is Mrs. Woolf's intelligence that recreates them.

There are dull passages in the book; the various
threads of the story are not gathered up, do not
become dramatic, until we are a quarter of the
way through, but once gathered up, they are never
released until the end; the growth and development of the complex of situations is steady.   One
character after another is caught into the action;
and it leaves none of them what they were before.
The easy course, the short cut, is never taken;
everything is worked out anew.   For comprehensiveness of understanding the author has never
surpassed *Night and Day*.   Yet we feel, regarding Mrs. Woolf's later works, that there is something lacking in it: the satisfaction of the artist
working within conditions shaped for herself.
The given conditions, it is true, are scrupulously
observed; but we feel them as a compulsion on the
writer; they are too impersonal; they have not
been resolved into a completely individual means
of expression.   *Night and Day* is a book which a
writer might execute, submitting to the form rather
than finding complete expression through it.

In the small volume of short shories, *Monday
or Tuesday*, the experimentation with form began

74

which later gave us *Jacob's Room* and *Mrs. Dalloway*. It is tentative, but lighter, more buoyant, than anything Mrs. Woolf had written before. *Jacob's Room* was a great advance; its plan was admirable; the recreation of a figure through memories and associations was a suggestive and perfectly valid device. The book contains several beautiful scenes, but it is not sure, like Mrs. Woolf's earlier and like her later work; it has a good deal of the sentimentality which so often comes out of the mind along with a first attempt to express something in it which has not been expressed before. When the artist tries to liberate his essential emotion towards experience, at first he is likely to liberate a great deal more along with it, until in this new kind of expression he learns to distinguish what is essential from what appears so. *Jacob's Room* has a more living quality than Mrs. Woolf's earlier work, but it is less critical. *Mrs. Dalloway* is the most characteristic work Mrs. Woolf has written. It is so unlike *Night and Day* that they can hardly be compared. It has not the earlier book's finely dramatic development or its intensity; but it is

75

more organic and in a more living sense, it is infinitely more subtle in its means, and it has on all its pages, as *Night and Day* had not, the glow of an indisputable artistic triumph. As a piece of expressive writing there is nothing in contemporary English fiction to rival it. Shades of an evanescence which one might have thought uncapturable, visual effects so fine that the eye does not take them in, that only in the memory are guessed at from the vibration they leave in passing, exquisitely graded qualities of sound, of emotion, of reverie, are in Mrs. Woolf's prose not merely dissected, but imaginatively reconstructed. All that in the earlier novels was analysed is resolved in *Mrs. Dalloway* into evocative images. There is nothing left of the stubborn explanatory machinery of the analytical novel. The material upon which the author works is the same as before, but it has all been sublimated, and, although the psychology is subtle and exact, no trace remains of the psychologist.

"And Clarissa had leant forward, taken his hand, drawn him to her, kissed him,—actually had felt his face on hers before she could down the brandishing of

silver-flashing plumes like pampas grass in a tropic gale
in her breast, which, subsiding, left her holding his hand,
patting his knee, and feeling as she sat back extraordinarily at ease with him and light-hearted—all in a clap
it came over her, If I had married him, this gaiety
would have been mine all day!"

How much more exact that is than analysis
could be! It is more exact, for the ebb and flow
of the imagery, the rhythm of the sentence, follow
the course of the emotion. First we have Clarissa's effusion of uncontrolled, blind emotion
evoking the image, "the brandishing of silver-
flashing plumes"; then the emergence from it to
a recognition of diurnal reality, reported rather
than described, "leaving her holding his hand,
patting his knee"; and finally in the accelerating
pace with which the sentence ends, the sudden
thought that if she had married him! It is exquisitely done.

Then there is the passage, too long to quote, in
which the sound of the bells of St. Margaret's,
which "glides into the recesses of the heart, buries
itself in ring after ring of sound, like something
alive which wants to confide itself, to disperse
itself, to be, with a tremor of delight, at rest," is

wedded in Peter Walsh's mind with the image of
Clarissa in her house, so that when "the sudden
loudness of the final stroke" comes, it seems to be
tolling "for death that surprised in the midst of
life, Clarissa falling where she stood in her drawing room. No! No! he cried. She is not
dead!" The mood that Mrs. Woolf catches here
is quite beyond the reach of the psychological,
analytical method; yet how perfectly it is con-
veyed. But more striking perhaps than either
of these is the description of Clarissa sewing her
green dress:

"Quiet descended upon her, calm, content, as her
needle, drawing the silk smoothly to its gentle pause,
collected the green folds together and attached them, very
lightly, to the belt. So on a summer's day waves collect,
overbalance, and fall; collect and fall; and the whole
world seems to be saying "that is all" more and more
ponderously, until even the heart in the body which lies
in the sun on the beach says too, That is all. Fear no
more, says the heart. Fear no more, says the heart,
committing its burden to some sea, which sighs collec-
tively for all sorrows, and renews, begins, collects, lets
fall. And the body alone listens to the passing bee; the
wave breaking; the dog barking, far away barking and
barking."

78

The transition here is daring, but wonderfully successful. While Mrs. Woolf is describing the falling of the waves, we never forget Clarissa sewing. The greater rhythm as it were accompanies the less, and it brings into the room where Clarissa is sitting its serenity and spaciousness. There is something in the ritual of sewing, a memory of another rhythm buried deep within it, which an image such as this, so unexpected, so remote, reveals to us. The rhythm of the prose is exquisitely graded; it has profited, one feels, as prose may, whether poetry may or not, by the experiments which have been made in vers libre: in the daring and fullness of the metaphors it has a remote indebtedness to Homer. There is no English prose at present, except Mr. Joyce's, which in subtlety and resource can be compared with it.

In a novel like *Mrs. Dalloway*, where the sensory impressions are so concretely evoked and are so much more immediate than they were before, a sort of rearrangement of the elements of experience insensibly takes place. In the traditional novel we have on the one hand the characters and on the other the background, each existing in a separate dimension, and the one generally more solid than the other. Sometimes the environment reacts strikingly on the characters, as for instance in *Wuthering Heights* and in Mr. Hardy's Wessex novels, but the reaction is not complex and continuous. It is indicated rather than treated, and the character and the background retain their peculiar values. But in *Mrs. Dalloway* they are more intimately connected; the one merges into the other; the character is suffused by the emanations of the things he sees, hears, feels; and almost inevitably what is presented is a complex of life, of which character and background are elements, both animate, rather than the living character stalking among inanimate things. The characters in *Mrs. Dalloway* are real; they have their drama; but the day and the properties of the day move with them, have their drama too; and we do not know which is the more real where all is real—whether the characters are bathed in the emanations of the day, or the day coloured by the minds of the characters. The result is less akin to anything else attempted

80

in the novel than to certain kinds of poetry, to poetry such as Wordsworth's which records not so much a general judgment on life as a moment of serene illumination, a state of soul. What nature is in *The Prelude* London is in *Mrs. Dalloway,* a living presence, a source of deep pleasure. The mood in which this presence is felt is perhaps the farthest removed from the dramatic, realistic mood. In *Night and Day* the chief thing is the action of the characters upon one another; in *Mrs. Dalloway* it is their intimate daily life with all the things which make it up and have reference only to themselves, but which are nevertheless more certainly their being than their actions are. Mrs. Woolf is not concerned in *Mrs. Dalloway* with the character, which is shown in action, in crises (and novels are consequently full of crises), but with the state of being. To give it its value she catches it at a particularly fortunate moment, at a moment of realization; but the means are justified and are, indeed, the normal means of art. To reveal character the novelist concentrates on crises, comic or tragic, leaving untouched the vast, inert mass of experience: in

81

concentrating on the daily existence when it is most significant Mrs. Woolf is in a different way obeying the same principle, the principle, indeed, of all imaginative art.

The Common Reader, in which Mrs. Woolf's mind deals with figures familiar to us all, shows it perhaps at its best. Her themes range from Chaucer to Conrad, from George Eliot to the Duchess of Newcastle, and in them all she shows the intelligence and practicality of temper of the critic. She has the informed enthusiasm which criticism should never lack but which is tending to disappear from it; her judgments have admirable breadth. The one important quality of the critic which she lacks is the power of wide and illuminating generalization. She holds the scales even, as she does between her characters in *Night and Day;* she uses her sensibility as she uses it in *Jacob's Room* and *Mrs. Dalloway.* It is the same mind, and we never doubt its competence to deal with anything which it fixes upon.

STEPHEN HUDSON

— V —

STEPHEN HUDSON

IF one were asked what distinguishes Mr. Stephen
Hudson's contribution to the literature of the age,
the reply might be that in his grasp of the motives
of action he shows a more complete mastery and
a greater sincerity than any one else.   The qualities in which he is peculiarly interested are those
which will have a decisive effect on the destiny of
a character: the qualities which betray Richard
Kurt into his first disastrous marriage and the
twenty years which follow it; the qualities which
make Tony an adventurer and take him with in-
corrigible ease into scrapes and out of them, until
at last he is tragically caught; the qualities which
make Elinor's course so triumphant, so hateful,
and so limited.   Action is never separated in his
novels, as it is in so many, from its results.   At
the moment of passion or of error his mind leaps

forward to the inevitable consequences; he apprehends immediately the change which a single action will impose upon future years; and it is this which makes his novels, with their bareness of outline, so dramatic. The simplest incidents he records are significant, for they carry on their surface the whole weight of a future. And as the actions of his characters imply the destiny which they are working out, so they presuppose all the qualities which have gone to produce them: the ruling passions which have in the past been expressed in actions of a like nature and thus have formed and consolidated a character, good or bad, weak or strong. Cause and effect are inescapable; every action, every impulse, has its relation; and it is Mr. Hudson's distinction to have apprehended this more completely than any other writer of our time. He has seen intensely this truth of necessity, psychological law, destiny, call it what we may; and, holding it, he has given to the characters he describes and the events he records a rare unconditionality, so that we feel they could be nothing but what they are, and that qualities no less than events are inexorable.

This sense of necessity, of cause and effect, is at the centre of Mr. Hudson's vision of life, and he has rejected more and more everything which is irrelevant to it. Accordingly the people he portrays are not so much characters as essences of character. When he describes Elinor and Tony he sets down nothing but the typical, nothing but those idiosyncrasies and acts which reveal the essential ego. He does this completely. Tony is self-subsistent not only in his ruling passions, but in his philosophy, which is an adumbration of these, and as inexorably necessitated. His character is consequently irrevocable, an organism operating by its own laws, which neither our love, nor our importunity, nor our opposition, can essentially change. At the centre of Elinor, in the same way, is a perfectly naïve egotism; but it is reinforced through the personality which by an inscrutable process it builds round itself to be its expression and its defence; so that even Elinor's thoughts are a part of her egotism, and she is incapable of thinking against herself. Where other writers convince us of the reality of their imaginary worlds by the employment of light and shade,

87

by making their characters act in apparent contradiction to themselves, but in a way to bring us
back once more to themselves, Mr. Hudson con-
vinces us by showing us in their passions, their
actions and their thoughts the same motive power.
Thus every expression, however noble, of a character of his will be determined by the limitations
of that character.   Even the virtues, to which people not necessarily sentimental sometimes attribute
an infinite effectuality, are in his novels effectual
only to an extent determined by the moral com-
plexion of the people who exercise them.   So
when Tony is actuated by affection for Richard
his measures are of no avail, for the decisive reason that the needs of the two brothers are different.
He acts out of himself and of all he has been so
purely, that there is more of himself than of virtue
in his virtues.   All Mr. Hudson's characters are
like Tony in this.   The gallery of characters in
Myrtle speak straight out of themselves, and their
utterance is limited by a complete, unconscious,
self-subsisting attitude to the world.   The paucity
of external characterization only makes the inner
characterization more definite.   Here as else-

where Mr. Hudson's imagination is occupied severely with essentials.

And for Mr. Hudson the essential things are the motives, the passions whose results, happy or disastrous, have an abiding effect. He writes about passions and sentiments only when they are motives, or insofar as they are motives. Of the passions in themselves in their diversity he has little to tell us, and although he does not avoid them, he indicates them briefly. He is so concentrated on their effects, on what they will bring rather than on what at the moment they present, that he selects from among their manifestations only those (and they are of course the essential ones) which will influence a whole tract of life, both essentially and externally. It is this that gives his novels their extraordinary economy, justifies that economy. It is this that enables him to produce in *Elinor Colhouse* an atmosphere of overhanging disaster, so that we feel in reading the book the shadow of the twenty years of suffering of which the incident it describes is to be the cause; for it is the lack of detailed attention to the passion itself, the nakedness with which the mo-

tives are revealed, that by such simple means
achieves this intensity. Everything in these
novels is oriented towards something which has
not yet emerged, and has as much the atmosphere
of a prelude as of a statement. Life is not moving, as we normally see it, towards no end that we
can foretell; it is moving rather towards a point
which is the point of reference of Mr. Hudson's
imagination, and is outside and beyond the part
of experience he is treating. This knowledge,
indirectly communicated to the reader, that in
writing of a particular time the author has the
full scope of a life in his imagination, both forward into the future and back into the past, enhances insensibly the inevitability of the different
parts, and gives as well a certain depth of background.

But if the feeling of consequences, of the certainties of the future, is by these indirect means
given so strongly in Mr. Hudson's novels, the
sense of the past, of causes, is given no less
strongly and by means as indirect. In *Prince
Hempseed* he began to exploit the resources of the
first person singular in narrative, and in *Tony*

and *Myrtle* he developed them. The beauty of
the first person singular is that, when it is used
as it should be, it implies at every moment, trans-
piring through the simplest statements, a whole
background, a whole life; and it does this the
more perfectly, the more apparently unpremedi-
tated the narrative, the less the narrator's eye is
fixed on one particular episode, the less obviously
interesting, even, the events are in themselves.
For when the events are so interesting in themselves that they occupy the centre of our attention,
the background—all the narrator has felt or seen
—falls away; he becomes mere function, a
narrator and nothing more, and his personality,
his very existence, become in a sense irrelevant,
for deprived of them he is a more perfect means
for his immediate purpose. He has no existence
except as the recorder of or the participator in the
action he describes, and it is by courtesy of it that
he exists, and not of his own right. He has no
past to throw its associations over the event, and
therefore no personality, for personality can only
be rendered in its growth or in its constancy, to
show either of which a direct or indirect reference

91

back is necessary. But having none of these things this questionable character has no serious artistic justification. When, to take a notorious example, Stevenson used the first person singular in *Treasure Island*, it was merely to make us believe more readily in the story by substituting for himself, a respectable writer living at the end of Victoria's reign, a boy who was on the spot and in the period. Tricks such as these are puerile, and if the reader accepts them as part of a game of make-believe between himself and the writer, he has to accept along with them a certain meaninglessness and triviality of enjoyment. But this is only one of the various false ways of exploiting the first person. The ordinary autobiographical novelist exploits it generally for its looseness, and to unburden his views on life upon us, rather than life itself. Mr. Hudson commits none of these errors. The form once chosen, he is almost unerring in his use of it. The personal monologue in which *Prince Hempseed, Tony* and *Myrtle* are written hardly ever falls into the set narrative piece which so readily arouses our suspicions; the events flow on, some of them apparently trivial,

some obviously important, and the reasons why
they are memorable are implicit in the emphasis
with which they are set down—are never explic-
itly or baldly stated. This monologue is neither
mere narrative nor a mere outpouring of memories bound together by threads of association. It
is rather a form in which the utterance of the
soliloquist is heightened, his uncritical memory
clarified and crystallized, his everyday personality replaced by the more essential personality
which self-knowledge reveals. This newly awak-
ened personality it is which tells us of the other
personality which existed before as its shadow,
seeing where it acted rightly and where wrongly,
and why. It gives distance to the presentation,
for looking back at what it once seemed to be, it is,
as it were, contemplating a different character.
The existence of this second more essential
personality it is which justifies so completely Mr.
Hudson's use of the first person; for through it
experience is not merely repeated, as it is in the
generality of autobiographical novels; it is as-
sayed.

But if the assaying of experience is the chief

function performed by the monologue as Mr. Hudson uses it, it has many other advantages. By means of it he provides that background to experience without which there can be no genuine art, and provides it indirectly, as the background in a work of art should be provided, to colour but not obscure or retard the action. Using it, he secures his effects by the simplest means. When, for instance, one of his monologists says in *Myrtle,* "They were all going down to the sea-side that August," there is a strange beauty of implied association in the banal statement; we add to it the necromancy of memory. Again Richard as a child was the witness of the strange scene between his mother and a visitor to the house. "As we went into the room, mamma was sitting on a chair with the back towards the door but Mr. Milosovitch was kneeling down in front of her. When we got inside, Uncle Fred suddenly stood still but I went on to mamma though I was looking at Mr. Milosovitch. What *was* he doing? Then he jumped up stiff and buttoned his coat up tight across his stomach. He stood up very straight

and held out his hands to me; I could see the blue
stone on his little fat finger. But I kept away
from him close to mamma and she held me to her.
No one said anything and presently Uncle Fred
went away." There by virtue of the fact that the
child does not know the meaning of the incident,
the scene is given a curious beauty, the beauty
which an incomprehensible ceremony might have
in which people we know are the actors, appearing suddenly as protagonists in a drama of which
we were ignorant. For those who can apprehend
them Mr. Hudson's work is full of effects such as
these. It is a characteristic of his art that in an
apparently banal scene he can give us something
which if it is not poetry opens a window on poetry.
And he does this not through any art of suggestion, but by being so exact and clear that our
imagination seizes the scene as if it were a concrete and inexplicable object, and is impelled to
act upon it as it acts on reality.

This condensed, eliminative, almost taciturn
art, has limitations; but a limitation in a work is
only bad when it is arbitrary and necessitated by

nothing in the character of the positive vision.
Mr. Hudson's limitations are definite, but they
are necessitated by his vision and his artistic purpose. They arise from the fact that being concerned with essentials, stating nakedly the motives
of his characters, he has to a great extent to ignore
that rich variety of manifestation which the motives create to be their disguise as much as their
expression. Certain writers, perhaps the majority, have concerned themselves in detail with the
disguises of the motives; have shown them tragically as illusion or in comedy as inconsistency,
cant, deceit; but Mr. Hudson is so impatient of
them that he takes us immediately to what under-
lies them, the particular object which by their
means the ego wishes to secure. This limits his
field of experience, but the limitation is organic,
it is a concentration; so that even when the chief
human passions are not exhaustively described
they are as actually present in our minds as if
they were. We feel them all the more strongly,
perhaps, because they are assumed; for assumptions are more incontestable than statements; and

the true value of economy in art is that, avoiding detailed description, it can convey intensely, and thus make it impossible for us to escape from, a solid mass of assumption. Mr. Hudson's work belongs to this rare and economical order.

ALDOUS HUXLEY

~ VI ~

ALDOUS HUXLEY

It is about five years since Mr. Huxley first became known to the public. A small volume of verse, *The Defeat of Youth,* had appeared before that, but it did not arouse much attention. *Limbo* did; and since its appearance Mr. Huxley has written eight books, comprising novels, short stories, a poem, and two volumes of essays. Productiveness such as this is unusual, but as remarkable as Mr. Huxley's industry has been his popularity. Most of his books have run into a third impression; even his essays and poems have been read. No other writer of our time has built up a serious reputation so rapidly and so surely; compared with his rise to acceptance that of Mr. Lawrence and Mr. Eliot has been gradual, almost painful. Mr. Huxley's public capitulated almost at the first stroke of his pen, and they have

101

been docile ever since. They have found in his works less a point of view than an affinity; they are as delighted with what he says as if a part of themselves, a part of themselves weary of humbug and the burdens it imposes, were saying it. To all those in difficulties, to everybody, a profound sense of relief is given if they are told at the right moment that what they take to be their soul is in reality their liver. The relief is great because the problem is at once simplified and its dimensions sensibly reduced. Mr. Huxley has been telling us in a variety of ways that it is our liver. It is a hit-or-miss diagnosis, as true, perhaps, as M. Coué's, but as one-sided, and essentially of the same order. It is also a peculiarly English kind of truth, for nowhere are prejudices and crotchets more really respected than in England.

But of the many writers who are saying that it is our liver no one says it so gracefully, so passionately, almost so entrancingly, as Mr. Huxley. Other writers of his generation, indeed most of them, have been disposed to reduce emotions, ideals, sentimentalities, to their elements, but no one else has done it so effectively and so amus-

102

ingly. Mr. Huxley is so effective partly because
he has the power of disengaging his mind as if it
were an impersonal instrument and letting it operate a little diabolically for its own purposes,
and partly because that mind is never too complex
for the immediate task, the pricking of an illusion. It does what it sets out to do; it desires to
do no more; it is extraordinarily effective and
completely without nuance. The style which is
its instrument is agreeable, lively, continuously
graceful, but it rarely attempts anything that
would be likely to strain its powers. Effectiveness, then, Mr. Huxley has in a striking degree.
He has a complete grasp of ways and means; he
is seldom in difficulties; he excels with ease in
every form he sets his hand to. But all this, one
feels, is achieved at the expense of something complex, immediate, and essential, for which he does
not seem to have striven. His style is supple,
natural, felicitous; but he has never expressed in
it a profound truth, nor described with it a living character. And if it be asked why he should
have done so the reply is that he has written novels
and in them has been perpetually obsessed by

certain types and by the philosophical problems
their lives present. He has called forth these
types and these problems; he has written a great
deal about them; but he has never really dealt
with them.

He has not done so because beneath all his freedom, his engaging licentiousness, of intellect,
there persists a certain conventionality, a certain
banality. In *Those Barren Leaves* he presents
the figure of a meretricious, unhappy, middle-
aged woman who thinks she is in love with a
young poet. For the imagination a figure such as
this held endless possibilities. Mr. Huxley had
the opportunity of exploiting these possibilities
and of revealing Mrs. Aldwinkle's soul. This,
however, he never attempts. He portrays Mrs.
Aldwinkle simply as a nuisance; the reaction of
his imagination to her is precisely the same as
the reaction of one of her own set might be. And
as he deals with Mrs. Aldwinkle he deals with
almost all his characters. His art is not one of
comprehension; it is one of exposure. He is content—and it is a sign of a certain naïveté of mind
—if he succeeds in stripping the make-believe

from people. In *Antic Hay* Gumbril, Lypiatt, Mercaptan, the egregious Rosie, are all stripped of their hypocrisies; but we are given no inkling of the sources from which these hypocrisies spring. Mr. Huxley dislikes hypocrisies with a fury which might be that of a moralist, but is not; the obvious truth is that he has not tried to understand them. For him they might be completely arbitrary, and spring from no cause more particular than the general turpitude of the human race. Because people are one thing and appear another, as they have always done and for their self-preservation must always do, he is enraged. But the objects of his indignation are nothing less than the laws of adaptation, the conditions of civilized existence, the attributes of human nature. All this makes Mr. Huxley as a novelist, as a portrayer of actual men and women, extraordinarily limited; it makes him as a satirist sometimes very penetrating. Not seeing complexities he cannot be deceived by them; and he maintains therefore through thick and thin, through everything perhaps but romantic love, his hold upon the ineradicable hypocrisy of the human race.

105

Yet often one is puzzled to tell why he does so. It is not because he is openly on the side of virtue, nor is it because he is fascinated, as Baudelaire was, by evil. He has the moral rage, without the morality, of a satirist; and although the effect is unintentional, sometimes he gives the impression of sitting on the fence, of a little irresolutely trying to make the worst of both worlds. We see him pursuing the perfectly worthless, the perfectly inoffensive Rosie through *Antic Hay* with an inexplicable hostility, in which there is a complete lack of moral purpose. Why should he do so? Obviously it is because his satire is not a criticism of hypocrisy, but a reaction to it. He does not set out to show hypocrisy in its essence and to trace its results, as he would be bound to do if he saw it objectively; he simply sets it down as an object of his dislike. He reacts to it in his characters; he reacts to it, also, in himself. This is a kind of honesty which is rare; but it is one which at the same time is in tune with this age and representative of it. This honesty is not discerning; it is content to convict us of the venial sins; and it takes a certain pleasure in thus hu-

miliating us. It is an honesty to certain immediate reactions each of which is apprehended in
a desert of banality, in the perfect waste left by
the disappearance of conceptions, ideals, orders,
which were accepted by other ages. It is so faith-
ful to the immediate reactions that it does not permit us to seek for their causes. And so, if there
is no philosophy, no attempt to account for the
world in general, in Mr. Huxley's books, neither
is there any psychology. And curiously enough
it is this that makes him such a perfect representative of one current of feeling of the age.
The crash of an order which was preparing before
the War, and which the War precipitated, does
seem to have left a generation who in their universal uncertainty doubt even such terms as the
world and the mind, are sceptical of any conclusions which may be drawn from the existence of
these things, and are prepared to accept only the
sensations they feel and the deceptions practised
by everybody to conceal them. No contemporary
writer has portrayed these sensations and seen
through these deceptions more clearly than Mr.
Huxley. He fills the scene completely, and what

is as essential, he does no more than fill it. There could not be a more perfect example of the writer of transition.

To be so completely of the period, to say unerringly what nine out of ten literate people wish to be said, finally to say it gracefully and wittily —this is in a sense its own reward, this is at the same time to be of service to one's generation if not to posterity. The writer who can do it must have talents of a high order; but he must also have definite limitations, must share as much in the blindness as in the knowledge of his period. He must see just what his contemporaries see, see it with no less knowledge, but also with no more profundity. He must never lift a veil from things; he must rather present everything in such a way that it has merely to be recognized. He must share without afterthought in the taste of the age; he must be as transitory, as onesided, as limited, as blind, as it. He must be all this, for this is the penalty exacted in exchange for the glance of immediate recognition, of instinctive sympathy, which his work provokes. And if we take almost

108

any scene from Mr. Huxley's novels we can see
how exactly these requirements are fulfilled, how
completely these limitations are observed. He is
presenting the histrionic Lypiatt, the unsuccessful
artist who has to talk loud to deceive himself:

Mrs. Viveash stood looking at the picture on the easel
(abstract again—she did not like it) and Lypiatt, who
had dropped his hand from her shoulder, had stepped
back the better to see her, stood earnestly looking at
Mrs. Viveash.

"May I kiss you?" he asked after a pause.

Mrs. Viveash turned towards him, smiling agonizingly,
her eyebrows ironically lifted, her eyes steady and calm
and palely, brightly inexpressive. "If it really gives
you any pleasure," she said. "It won't, I may say, to
me."

"You make me suffer a great deal," said Lypiatt, and
said it so quietly and unaffectedly, that Myra was almost startled; she was accustomed, with Casimir, to
noisier and more magniloquent protestations.

"I'm very sorry," she said; and really she felt sorry.
"But I can't help it, can I?"

"I suppose you can't," he said. "You can't," he repeated, and his voice had now become the voice of Pro-
metheus in his bitterness. "Nor can tigresses." He
had begun to pace up and down the unobstructed fair-

109

way between his easel and the door; Lypiatt liked pacing
while he talked. "You like playing with the victim,"
he went on; "he must die slowly."

Reassured, Mrs. Viveash faintly smiled.

That is a fair example of Mr. Huxley's method,
and how telling it is, but how perfectly on the surface, how crude even. The essence of this satire
is that Lypiatt is not for a moment understood; if
he were, another kind of satire would be necessary
to do justice to him. He is not a human being
with innumerable interests, with many masks, and
with a past to explain them. He is rather one set
of interests only, one mask which never varies and
has no existence before and after his appearance
in the book. His life begins at forty and continues for a few weeks; apart from these he is a
perfect blank, an inexplicable void. In Mr.
Huxley's novels we are given a succession of impressions of people we have never met before, with
whom we never become intimate, and who are
never explained. The author tears their masks
away, but there is nothing underneath. The pro-
longed scrutiny which would discern variety in
these figures and would thus humanize them he

110

never casts in their direction. He is completely in the present, and he finds it exciting, exasperating, amusing. The humours, the lusts, the hypocrisies, the snobberies—he discovers them all there, and he portrays them. But they remain disembodied. They are not qualities belonging to specific characters and coloured by that fact; they are general attributes of human nature.

All this, then, makes Mr. Huxley as a novelist a very unsatisfying, almost an incongruous figure. We feel there is no necessity why he should have chosen the novel rather than another form for what he has to say. It provides him with a loose frame for his intellectual fantasies; and in that frame his ideas are more piquant perhaps than they would be without it. But it is an improvisation, not a form; it has a utilitarian, but not an æsthetic, reason for existing. And in choosing it Mr. Huxley has certainly lost more than he has gained. For the fantastic little essays and dialogues—"the delicious little middles"—for which his stories are chiefly read, lose a great deal by being put in the mouths of people whom we find shoddy, ill-made, second-rate, and in any case

much less interesting than their author himself,
who is in reality speaking. Mr. Huxley's work
consists essentially in a running argument, sometimes ingenuous, sometimes ironical, with himself.
But he interposes between us and this interesting
dispute his Gumbrils, Lypiatts, Mercaptans, and
worse; and they are tiresome; they stand between
us and the theme; they make the author's utterance one degree more false. Unfortunately
there is no getting over the bad effects of an error
of this kind. Mistakes in the choice of form are
fatal; they spring either from a lack of artistic
conscience, or from a debility of imagination; and
in either case the writer, unable to see how things
will work out, is inevitably driven to mere improvisation. Mr. Huxley has intelligence, fancy
and wit, but little imagination; and he has chosen
the prose form in which imagination is most indis-
pensable. When he resigns it for the purely
fantastic, the purely intellectual, as in the short
story of the dwarf in *Chrome Yellow,* we feel immediately that his talents are heightened and that
his work becomes original and serious. In that
story his intellectual fancy is not an irrelevance,

as it is in his novels; it is an animating principle. This kind of story may well be the form which suits his gifts. He has found it once; he may yet achieve something large in it. As it is, it outweighs everything else he has written, and is the best criticism that exists of the remainder of his work.

LYTTON STRACHEY

VII

LYTTON STRACHEY

"THE art of biography," said Mr. Strachey in the preface to *Eminent Victorians,* "seems to have fallen on evil times in England. . . . With us the most delicate and humane of all the branches of the art of writing has been relegated to the journeyman of letters: we do not reflect that it is perhaps as difficult to write a good life as to live one. Those two fat volumes, with which it is our custom to commemorate the dead—who does not know them, with their ill-digested masses of material, their slip-shod style, their tone of tedious panegyric, their lamentable lack of selection, of detachment, of design?" The judgment passed there on biography might as justly have been passed on the main branch of modern literature, the novel. There, too, would have been found "ill-digested masses of material," a "slip-shod

117

style," a "lamentable lack of selection, of detachment, of design." When Mr. Strachey wrote, the novel had lost its autonomy, its inner centre, and the laws springing from that which determine æsthetic form. It had lost its laws, and sought laws outside itself, in the subject-matter which it treated, in political and moral concepts. The result was that it had ceased to be an æsthetic phenomenon and had become very largely a social one. Anything whatever could be called a novel which treated of manners, just as anything whatever could be called a biography which gave information about a personality. It was Mr. Strachey's distinction in reinstating biography as an art to draw attention to the formlessness of literature generally. He did this in common with writers very unlike him, for whom he could have had little sympathy: with such writers as Mr. Joyce and Mr. Eliot. Progress in literary appreciation is very slow; but now, at any rate, it is becoming less general to judge a novel by its subject-matter, or a biography by the industry of the biographer.

In his attempt to capture biography for art Mr.

118

Strachey started with an immense advantage over the novelist: for biography was neither regarded as an art nor expected to be one. His problem was therefore admirably simple, and his success correspondingly clear and unmistakable. *Eminent Victorians* was a demonstration more victoriously obvious than anyone could have produced in the confused field of fiction of the difference between art and the immense body of writing which is not art. It provided almost immediately a new criterion for the judgment of biography. People were suddenly dissatisfied with the biographer in the old style who avoided with equal skill tragedy and comedy, actual and artistic truth. And they appreciated anew the excellence of art, when they found it in such an unexpected place.

In *Eminent Victorians* Mr. Strachey did two things for biography: he humanized it by irony, he gave it form. He went out in search not of great figures and noble characters, but of human nature, and he always found it. Having found it, he set it out in his own terms. All his characters passed through his eighteenth-century work-

119

shop, and emerged in the ironically appropri-
ate costumes he had devised for them. They
emerged, if not in their own shape, then in some
shape which revealed it. For the time being their
author's puppets, they played over again the game
which they had played far more intensely, sometimes in tears and agony, in the actual world.
Mr. Strachey held the strings which moved this
puppet play, and they were constantly being
manipulated, but very rarely did we catch sight
of them. The figures seemed to be going through
the ballet of their own lives, a ballet simplified
and stylized to the last detail; and it was only in
the conventionalization of the costumes and attitudes that one recognized the choreographer.

There was drama in that spectacle, but it was
a drama which had taken place a long time before,
and existed now only as a memory and a conscious
play. The figures "remembered" for the hun-
dredth time when they had to make such and such
a gesture, when they had to laugh, weep, show
lively apprehension, anticipation, repentance,
doubt, affection. They did not feel; they imitated

the passions, sorrowful or happy, which happened to come their way in the game.

It is this effect of distance and illusion which gives Mr. Strachey's work its rare poetic quality, and makes him a distinguished artist. He writes in two moods: the consciously ironical in which he satirizes the pretensions and hypocrisies of men, and the involuntarily ironical in which he sees the drama of existence as a transitory, illusory process which has happened so often that it has now but an apparent reality. Only where his deliberate irony is quiescent does this more profound irony come into play. His portrait of Arnold of Rugby, for example, is excellent satire; but his portraits of Manning, Florence Nightingale, and Victoria are something more. *Queen Victoria* was commended for being less ironical than *Eminent Victorians,* but the truth was that in it Mr. Strachey's irony had only released the lesser themes of the satirist to seize upon life itself. With the abrogation of his conscious gift for ironical presentation the true bias of his profoundly ironical mind was revealed, and the

121

complete compass of his imagination released.

The strange thing is that through this irony he arrived, without formulating them, at conclusions not unlike those of men for whom one can detect in his works no sympathy: the metaphysicians, mystics, and saints. Life as Mr. Strachey portrays it is an illusion; he can portray it as nothing else; and his work is most profound precisely where the sense of illusion is most unmistakably given: where he shows Manning mounting the little back stair of the Vatican or walking in state to Westminster; where he describes the distant and tiny figure of Gordon standing on the toy ramparts of Khartoum, gazing over a desert which only to him is illimitable; where he records the remote sorrows, domestic and State, of the little woman who sat on England's throne. We remember the incidents in his books which destiny seems to be arranging for their unconscious effect: Newman weeping outside the house at Littlemore, Disraeli bearing flowers to the Queen. These incidents, trivial or moving, have a significance almost symbolical, as if in them the complete essence of a character were ex-

pressed. If a choreographer were to put these
characters in a ballet he would fix them in precisely the postures Mr. Strachey has fixed them
in. A mystic would do the same. On the life of
this world a complete scepticism and a profound
mysticism may come to the same conclusions.

For the rarefied drama of his biographies Mr.
Strachey has a style in appearance artificial, but
in essence transparently simple, with the arresting simplicity, once more, of the ballet. It has
been called an eighteenth-century style, but it is
something far more rare, an echo of the eighteenth
century, with a remoteness, a complete absence of
matter of fact, of which the eighteenth century did
not dream. At his best this style gives his work
an impressive feeling of distance; at his second-
best it seems both to temper and emphasize his
irony: very seldom does it ring false. It is a
perfect means when he is writing of Manning or
of anyone else who has lived a great number of
times in history, and, always suffering from the
same scruples, has always done the same things
for the satisfaction of the same ambitions. These
men, who are regularly recurring historical figures

rather than persons, Mr. Strachey's style seems made for; its conventionalization and ceremoniousness seem to generalize every manifestation of human nature, to show in the particular act the invariable form to which it belongs, and in every attempt to disobey, a disguised conformity. One sometimes feels that in Mr. Strachey's mind there is a mathematical formula for certain types; for Manning, for example, and Arnold, and Victoria. When these recur in history they will inevitably do certain things and deceive themselves about them in certain ways; and Mr. Strachey's intellectual pleasure is to perch them for a moment on the fence, knowing mathematically on which side they must fall. The drama of his characters is in moments like these, which seem to be free, but are not. He is interested in the norm, and while he enjoys deviations from it his main pleasure is in the inevitable return from the deviation. He is delighted by the things which always manage to happen, against every probability but the chief one.

He succeeds with the rule; he does not always succeed with the exception. His Manning is admirable; his Gordon is unconvincing. For the exception is a man who avoids those universally symbolical gestures which fit so well the historical figure. He is a man who does not seek worldly success but something else, and to whom comes not success or resignation, but tragedy. He can leave a symbolical formula only for the poet, not for the biographer. Gordon was bound to play havoc with the delicate, resourceful, but essentially limited technique of *Eminent Victorians*. There are admirable things in Mr. Strachey's sketch of Gordon, but never does one feel that he puts his finger on the inner spring of Gordon's actions. Gordon did not suit him as a subject, simply because he could not believe in the things in which Gordon believed, and could not understand a sincere belief in them. To others who "believed," but whose spring of action was not their belief— to Victoria, Manning, Arnold—he showed understanding and sympathy. For hypocrisy is a genuine manifestation of that human nature which the wise man tolerates and enjoys; and to a touch of nature Mr. Strachey will pardon anything. But Gordon was not a man demanding toleration, and one feels that Mr. Strachey was a little non-plussed by him. He would not be human in Manning's way. He upset the mathematical formula.

Yet he is perhaps the only figure in the gallery to whom the biographer has been unjust; for impartiality is one of Mr. Strachey's chief virtues. Every stroke of irony in his books is weighed not for its effectiveness but for its justice; and accordingly every stroke tells. He conventionalizes his themes, certainly; he expresses them in terms of his eighteenth-century intellect and his modern imagination; but he does not falsify them. He gains more in effect by ignoring an obvious advantage than Mr. Philip Guedalla, for example, gains by seizing it. He has the eighteenth-century instinct for the judgment which can be reasonably defended, and the eighteenth-century knowledge that an inessential piece of cleverness is always foolish, for it will be found out. A witty writer, there is very little of his wit that can be detached without detaching a valuable piece of characterization or injuring a perfectly serious judgment.

He seems at first glance to be completely out-

126

side the current of modern literature; and a clever writers calls him a Voltaire who has reached the age of two hundred odd years. There is little resemblance between the author of *Queen Victoria* and the author of *La Pucelle*. Mr. Strachey's sensibility is modern; his imagination is romantic; only by his cool rationality does he belong to the eighteenth century. His *Cardinal Manning* and *Queen Victoria* would have appeared very novel if not quite incomprehensible to Dr. Johnson; their sceptical imagination and compassionate irony would have disturbed the lexicographer's mind. The truth is that Mr. Strachey has a very modern temperament and sensibility, and that he would be more completely at a loss than almost any other writer if he were transported into the eighteenth century. If he appears out of place in our time it is not because his intelligence is unmodern; it is because his temperament is unique. He is an inimitable writer, but he belongs as certainly to this age as Lamb did to his.

T. S. ELIOT

VIII

T. S. ELIOT

THERE is probably no writer of our time who has said more things about the art of literature which are at once new and incontrovertible than Mr. T. S. Eliot. He has written very little. His criticism is contained in *The Sacred Wood,* a small book, and in *Homage to Dryden,* a still smaller one. With every subject he has attempted he has only made a beginning, said a few pregnant or subversive words, and stopped. His criticisms of Dante, Blake, Swinburne, and Dryden have the appearance of footnotes. The series of essays in *The Sacred Wood* on the problems of criticism end with a remarkable economy of generalization. Even in essays which are more full, in those on Ben Jonson and Marvell, Mr. Eliot seems to be filling in the few strokes needed to complete a portrait rather than drawing an original one himself.

This impression of incompleteness is largely misleading. It is only when one tries to discover what essential aspect of Jonson's talent has been left untreated in Mr. Eliot's essay that one realizes how nearly complete it is. His prose is deceptive because in it he exercises continuously the faculty, rare in our time, for always saying more than he appears to say. In his essays he seems most of the time to be concerned with minor points, but he is in reality concerned always with essential ones. His critical method consists in pressing a small lever and in thereby releasing an unsuspectedly heavy weight. His essays are full of sentences such as "Swinburne's intelligence is not defective, it is impure," or "We have no prose to compare with Montaigne or Rabelais": of observations which do not appear important, but turn out to be those on which a really just generalization would be based. Accordingly his criticisms continuously grow in interest: they are among the few written in our time to which one can go back and find something which one perusal, or two, did not yield. In one way Mr. Eliot is the most complete critic of our time. What he does choose to say he says almost unassailably. He rarely sets down an opinion without being conscious of all that has already been said in favour of or against it, and his final pronouncement is not only something new, of the same solidity, the same order, as what has been said already; it is at once a summing-up and a revaluation. No one writing to-day has a more strong sense of tradition. He has written profoundly of it in his essay *Tradition and the Individual Talent,* saying that we are not merely judged by tradition but that we also modify it; that by adding one new work of art to those which constitute tradition we do something which is enough to change, however slightly, its character; and that thus tradition is a thing which is forever being worked out anew and recreated by the free activity of the artist.

Admirable and profound words—yet why is it that in spite of them Mr. Eliot always appears to us to underestimate the free character of tradition, the fact that in its living perpetuation it gives

133

the artist his proper liberty, and is not so much a
thing to be submitted to or imposed as to be discovered and welcomed? The influence of tradition on Mr. Eliot's criticism is not to make it
uniformly bold and comprehensive, but more
generally to make it cautious. He often draws
back where a genuinely classical writer, a writer
in the full stream of tradition, knowing the dangers, seeing the raised eyebrows of all the past
and hearing the warnings of the present, would
have gone on. Mr. Eliot feels answerable to
tradition for every judgment he makes: but this
accepted responsibility, while it gives his criticism
weight, sometimes makes it curiously timid.
Thus, if his enthusiasms are never wild, his un-
derstatements sometimes are. One is struck by
the sheer oddity when he describes Goethe's *Faust*
as "a very able and brilliant poem," and when,
·admitting that a few "many-sided" men must
"probably" be conceded to history, he adds:
"Perhaps Leonardo da Vinci is such." It is as
easy to lose one's sense of proportion through excessive caution as through excessive rashness. In
these instances Mr. Eliot's caution becomes

mechanical, and functions where it is not needed
and has no meaning.

But if his criticism is sometimes weighed down
by his sense of tradition, it is also enriched and
enlightened by it. His great gift as a critic is that
of seizing the artistic source and justification of a
convention, the necessity in a poem of elements
which may appear artificial, the real virtue of a
school, the essential law of a work of art. He
makes every work live while he considers it, for
he sees its articulations, the necessity for them,
and their living functioning. Thus, though at
times he may appear to be concerned with crafts-
manship alone, he is in reality concerned with the
organic structure, trying to discover whether it is
a living body or merely an agglomeration of
parts. He does not show a writer's "qualities,"
therefore, but the principles of his art. The reward of this difficult and concentrated way of approach is that in Mr. Eliot's criticism the work of
art, stripped of all incidentals, shines with its own
light, and that in an immediate way the artistic
problem is brought before us. In penetration,
knowledge, intuitive apprehension of the inner

laws of a poem, Mr. Eliot deserves to be ranked with the chief English critics.

His criticism has had a considerable influence on younger writers: his poetry has had perhaps even a greater influence. But as a poet his influence has not been in the same direction as his influence as a critic. The author of *The Sacred Wood* and *Sweeney Erect* is obviously a writer of contrasts. Certainly the poet in Mr. Eliot sets out to obey the critic. The idea, for example, that since the Elizabethan era poetry has been losing its complexity, its richness, contrast, surprise, subtlety—a favourite idea of Mr. Eliot's, and a very fruitful one—is as clearly to be seen in his poetry as in his criticism. His poetry does attempt to restore some of the psychological richness of Elizabethan poetry, to be more full and diverse, to attain a new and more vigorous beauty. But in aiming at one thing it in reality achieves another. It has not the fullness and suppleness, the mixture of extreme refinement and natural coarseness of Elizabethan poetry. These elements are present, it is true; *The Waste Land* has

136

extreme refinement and extreme coarseness; but they are not harmoniously and variously combined, producing a diversity of rich effects; they are set down side by side, in contrast, not in combination. Mr. Eliot's poetry is in reality very narrow, and in spite of its great refinement of sensibility, very simple. In the main it is a statement of two opposed experiences: the experiences of beauty and ugliness, of art and reality, of literature and life. To Mr. Eliot in his poetry these are simple groups of reality; their attributes remain constant; they never pass into one another; and there is no intermediate world of life connecting and modifying them. The plan of the early *Sweeney Among the Nightingales* is the same as that of *The Waste Land*. The raw fact and the remembered vision, the banal and the rare, the crude and the exquisite, reality and art, are set down side by side.

> The circles of the stormy moon
>   Slide westward toward the River Plate,
> Death and the Raven drift above
>   And Sweeney guards the horned gate.

Gloomy Orion and the Dog
    Are veiled; and hushed the shrunken seas;
The person in the Spanish cape
    Tries to sit on Sweeney's knees.

This is the simple contrast which one finds again
and again in Mr. Eliot's poetry; and all the poet's
admirable subtlety of mind is directed not to vary-
ing the contrast, but to making it as violent as
possible. This he effects in two ways: by releasing the contrast suddenly at the moment when it
will produce the maximum shock, and by refining
the passages of formal beauty and psychological
obscenity until their juxtaposition has an element
of horror. The former device is unworthy a
serious poet; the latter has yielded Mr. Eliot many
exquisite lines and a few passages expressing a
curious mood, not of despair, nor of mere depres-
sion, but of something which seems to combine
both and to pass beyond them:—

A rat crept softly through the vegetation
Dragging its slimy belly on the bank,
While I was fishing in the dull canal
On a winter evening round behind the gashouse,
Musing upon the king my brother's wreck,
And on the king my father's death before him.

138

It is in passages such as this that Mr. Eliot has attained nearest to beauty in his portrayal of actual experience; for in his passages of pure beauty the inspiration is generally literature. This passage has the same quality as the earlier

> The sable presbyters approach
> The avenue of penitence;
> The young are red and pustular,
> Clutching piaculative pence.

It is the artistic realization of what Mr. Eliot failed to express when he wrote:—

> The red-eyed scavengers are creeping
> From Kentish Town and Golder's Green.

It is, in short, the expression of a mood in which a hatred of squalor disguises a certain pleasure in squalor. This mood is not uncommon, as most people would have to admit if they had Mr. Eliot's courage; and, could it be grasped with all its implications—as Baudelaire grasped similar moods —it would no doubt be found to be profoundly significant. But Mr. Eliot does not grasp its implications. His presentation of it is at once bold and timid—it is inconclusive, and, one feels,

139

deliberately so. The mood is not pulled out into the light frankly and cleanly as one of Mr. Eliot's Elizabethans, for instance, would have pulled it out. And it is for this reason that his poetry is sometimes displeasing, as all things fragmentary and unrealized are. It is not displeasing because the poet expresses his anguish so fully that we cannot endure it, but because he does not express it fully enough. For when the sense of the pain of life is fully expressed, with nothing kept back, with no self-protecting veil between the poet and his suffering, it brings release. And release Mr. Eliot's poetry rarely attains. It is not false nor shallow, but it is inconclusive: it lacks immediacy and importance. It expresses an attitude to life, not a principle of life. The difference between

> *Non val cosa nessuna*
> *I moti tuoi, nè di sopiri è degna*
> *La terra. Amaro e noia*
> *La vita, altro mai nulla; e fango è il mondo,*

to quote a poet who had even more than Mr. Eliot's gloom, and

> Then how should I begin
> To spit out all the butt-ends of my days and ways?

is a difference fundamentally in seriousness. As
a poet Mr. Eliot lacks seriousness. He is bitter,
melancholy, despairing, but he is not serious.
There are moments when seriousness is given him.
It is his in the two beautiful and terrible verses
which conclude *Sweeney Among the Nightin-*
gales:—

> The host with someone indistinct
>   Converses at the door apart,
> The nightingales are singing near
>   The Convent of the Sacred Heart,
>
> And sang within the bloody wood
>   When Agamemnon cried aloud,
> And let their liquid droppings fall
>   To stain the stiff, dishonoured shroud.

But when that seriousness is absent what is left?
Not, indeed, a pose, but an attitude which will
seem in another few years as obsolete as Byron's
or Musset's seems to us now. It is, curiously
enough, an attitude very like theirs. Disdain
for life, loneliness of soul, the sardonic gesture,
the mysterious sorrow—all these are in Mr. Eliot's
poetry. They are also in Mr. Huxley's novels,

141

they have been called the spirit of the age, and it is impossible to take them seriously.

But although Mr. Eliot's work has not the fullness and seriousness of great poetry, it is something beautifully finished and quite unique. In it an anguished vision of the world is expressed in light verse. In all Mr. Eliot's finest poems, in the various poems about Sweeney, *Burbank with a Baedeker, Whispers of Immortality, The Love Song of Prufrock,* the mood and the treatment are deliberately too trivial for the theme. That is Mr. Eliot's method, and it is one which can admirably render a deep loathing for life. Grief appears somehow both intensified and belittled when it is expressed in the most artificial terms the poet can find; disgust assumes the importance of a conviction steadily held when pains are taken to discover the most polished formula for it.

But though I have wept and fasted, wept and prayed,
Though I have seen my head (grown slightly bald)
    brought in upon a platter,
I am no prophet—and here's no great matter;
I have seen the moment of my greatness flicker,

And I have seen the eternal Footman hold my coat, and
    snicker,
And in short, I was afraid.

There everything is underlined, every word is
written for effect, and we are intended to know
it. In its hint of theatricality this poetry is like
Heine's, but the theatricality is not ironical, as
Heine's was. Heine could only have spoken of
the eternal Footman with his tongue in his cheek;
Mr. Eliot does so with perfect seriousness. His
theatricality is always meant: he may often appear, but he very rarely is, ironical. His utterance is a sort of elegant bombast used sincerely;
and the real distinction of his "sable presbyters,"
his Princesses Volupine, his Grishkins, is that
they are not what they look, that is, creatures of a
melodramatic fancy, but seriously intended symbols to body forth a genuine vision of life. Very
few poets have used symbolism of a similar kind
for a similar purpose, and to have done so estab-
lishes Mr. Eliot's originality. At the same time
it is clear that in these symbols a great variety of
meanings could not be expressed. And although

143

his symbolism makes Mr. Eliot's poetry arresting piquant, unique, it makes him fatal to imitators and till now a poet of inferior range. The instrument of expression he has forged would not serve for a great poet, and could not be used by an unskilful one.

EDITH SITWELL

～ IX ～

EDITH SITWELL

In most romantic poetry there is a certain duality
of vision, a deviation, imperceptible or violent,
from the normal way of seeing things which has
the effect of making us see them more intensely.
In such lines as

> I'll show you where the white lilies grow
> On the banks o' Italie,

the deviation, though marvellously effective, is
slight. It is more violent in *Tyger, Tyger,* but
it is violent, too, in poetry more purely romantic,
such as

> The moon doth with delight
> Look round her when the heavens are bare,

or, still a better example,

> *Die marmor Bilder stehn und sehn mich an.*

Here use and convention, it is true, blind us to the violence; we feel it, indeed, as a natural effect of intensity of vision; but none the less this kind of perception is by classical standards unnatural, abnormal. Its effectiveness depends finally on the fact that when an object is seen in a certain way it automatically evokes its opposite. In lines such as these poetry is obeying a law which operates in all our minds, the law which makes a cataract appear at times to have an intensity of motionlessness which inanimate things lack, and rocks to come to life. The poet having reached the end, as it were, of the immobility of the statue, is compelled to make it breathe and move, for the unconditionality of its motionlessness can only become comprehensible to him through an evocation of something else as unconditional. Thus it is when we see the cataract as motionless that by a return upon itself of the mind we realize most intensely its swiftness and power. Romantic poetry, which has always striven for an absolute and therefore inhuman vision of things, has tended to see objects in this violently dualistic way.

To this poetry of opposites, in which motion-

lessness is described by motion, the living by the
inanimate, the best of Miss Sitwell's work belongs.   What is it, then, that makes that work so
unfamiliar and new?   What distinguishes it from
romantic poetry in general?—for the difference is
obviously great.   One may perhaps describe this
difference best by saying that Miss Sitwell em-
ploys the romantic method logically, deliberately
and all the time, where the purely romantic poet
used it only when a difficulty in his theme dic-
tated it, and there was no other way out.   Whether
she is intensely moved or not the transformation
of the dynamic into the static, of the audible into
the visible, and so forth, takes place; it happens as
if by a natural process.   Goethe describes the
statues as standing and gazing, because no other
terms could at the moment have rendered them,
but when Miss Sitwell speaks of country gentle-
men who

> from their birth
> Like kind red strawberries root in earth,

she is not seeing the object so intensely that there
is only this to be said; she is simply seeing it in
149

a different way from us. It is as if the senses
were operating in a new manner and changing all
the perceptions; and Miss Sitwell does claim that
a re-orientation of the senses is taking place. But
while the perceptions of this re-oriented sensibility
are original and strange, and arrest our attention,
it does not follow that the world they describe is a
new world; it may as well be the world we know
rendered in a different set of terms.

This is the question which will inevitably be
asked about any general transposition of the perceptions. We feel it to be arbitrary, a change
made without explanation, rather than a progression which explains itself. We accept Goethe's
line; we recognize that here he overcame an
obstacle by carrying his theme into a new dimension: the progression is both extraordinary and
inevitable. But in Miss Sitwell's transposition of
imagery we do not feel that an obstacle has
been overcome, but simply that the vision has been
shifted; and when she writes of trees "hissing like
green geese" or of

> The insipid, empty-tasting fruits
> Of summer giggling through the rounded leaves,

she does not necessarily make the world more real or comprehensible to us. We receive an excellent impression, but one which leaves the object, on the whole, where it was.

If the originality of Miss Sitwell's poetry consisted entirely in a general transposition of imagery it would not be essentially interesting, for it would be too easily explained. To conventionalize one's vision is a short-cut, but it is a short-cut of the intellect, not of the imagination, and it tends finally to fetter the imagination. That Miss Sitwell has taken the short-cut sometimes is undeniable, and some of her poetry is a poetry of method rather than of imagination. But at its best that poetry has the flash of divination, the sudden view of fresh worlds, which art exists to give us. When that happens in her poetry the uniform transposition does definitely heighten the effect. All imaginative creation has the power to astonish us, but when it takes place on an unfamiliar plane the achievement seems somehow more absolute; if we cannot quite comprehend it, neither can we gainsay it. We are moved strangely by this new and unanticipated world;

151

we feel it as a world of possibility, a metaphysical parallel to the actual world, which will last as long as it. So while Blake's tiger is not the tiger our eyes see, his image of the tiger makes us comprehend it better than any more realistic description, however exact, could have done. Here, too, a principle somewhat analogous to the principle of opposites comes into play. The poet having intensely contemplated the actual, begets an ideal form corresponding to it, which is really an adumbration of it in the realm of the possible, a demonstration which gives us an unique sense of its truth and necessity. For if it is real here, in a world of possibility, we feel that there is something absolute in its reality.

This peculiar kind of imagination, mystical and romantic, is Miss Sitwell's highest gift. When she writes of

> Adder flames shrieking slow,

when she says that

> like a gold-barred tiger, shade
> Leaps in the darkness,

or describes how

like the lovely light gazelles
Walking by deep water wells,
Shadows past her mirrors fleet,

the entities she describes exist in another world, they are ideal or magical forms; but they correspond in some way to reality and illuminate it. We see it anew.

The imagination in general animates things; the mystical imagination not only animates them, but makes them move, and tends to personify them. In this it is very like the imagination of children; and like most mystical poets Miss Sitwell has a childlike clarity of perception. One feels that her proper names, her Myrrhines, Jemimas, Marthas and Debs, are real or imagined names remembered from childhood. Like these they are not merely names; they are magical charms operating by the pure value of their syllables. *The Wooden Pegasus* recalls the rocking horse in the nursery; *The Sleeping Beauty* is the old children's tale. In these poems the colours of things are seen as if they were not colours merely, but things in themselves. They are seen, as a child sees them, so distinctly that, for in-

stance, the squares of colour on an object seem
to be independent entities; and a coloured box is
not one thing but a crowd of things. These
colours are clear and unmixed; each by itself fills
the attention. And as the colours are independent
of the object, so the object is independent of us.
An apple is hard, like painted wood. It is
absolute, as everything tends to be when we see
it for the first time and before the mind has begun to relate it to this and that. It is not a fruit
to be eaten, but an entity to be recognized. And
to light, shadow, rain, wind, grass, Miss Sitwell's
imagination accords the same autonomy; and like
everything which we regard as independent and
yet relevant to us, they are in greater or lesser degree personified.

This bright and childlike vision, this faculty
for seeing each particular thing so clearly that
nothing else is seen, is one of Miss Sitwell's dis-
tinguishing virtues, but it is also her chief defect. The faculty which she lacks—and it is a
very important one—is the faculty of correlation.
And so the vision is rarely seized completely; it
is implicit, and implicit only. When Blake says:

154

The human dress is forgèd iron,
The human form a fiery forge,
The human face a furnace sealed,
The human heart its hungry gorge,

he is not strictly comprehensible, but he is saying all that he desires to say. But we do not know immediately, sometimes we only know by reasoning, what Miss Sitwell wishes to say. The labour of synthesizing her intuitions, of making herself intelligible to herself, she has hardly undertaken; yet this is simply the art of poetic articulation. In her best poetry the separate intuitions are absolutely pure, but the connection which must needs exist between them is not seized; and instead of the beautiful relevance of parts which we find in great poetry we are left with something like a disintegration of structure.

And this defect, unfortunately, involves another. A world of things seen for the first time is exclusively a world of objects, and objects in themselves are monotonous; it is the infinity of relations between them that gives them inexhaustible interest. Through these their attributes are revealed, in adaptation, expression, communication.

Without these they remain only half real; and in the bulk of Miss Sitwell's poetry things do remain in this state. One distinction she admits: things are either dynamic or static. But even so the imagery is monotonous, for of a static thing one can say only that it stays, of a process only that it proceeds. The state of immobility, the state of change—to these Miss Sitwell has given a strange and oppressive significance; but only in her later poetry has she transcended this purely inhuman vision, translating the mystical, undifferentiated emotion of horror into the human and discerning emotion of pity. In *The Sleeping Beauty* that translation began; in some of the poems in *Troy Park* it is almost complete. She is concerned in these no longer with a process, but rather with a drama. Her first picture of the world, consisting of colours moving or still, is particularized here; organic and conscious forms appear in it. What the ultimate result of this development may be no one can say; but for poetry such as Miss Sitwell's it was the inevitable next step.

Of that poetry as it stands one can say, therefore, only a few things; one can hardly formulate a complete criticism. No poet has moved more bewilderingly than Miss Sitwell in worlds not realized. We recognize that these worlds are real: the accent, the vividness of the flashes in which they are revealed, tell us that. But when we seem to be on the verge of comprehension suddenly everything changes; time, space, and causality vanish: it is as if appearance were being shattered and rearranged by a continuously exploding bomb. No sooner has the imagination begun to build round one image than it is presented with another to which in vain it seeks to adapt itself. But in the seizing of those moments, so vivid, so beautiful, so strangely juxtaposed, Miss Sitwell's great powers are shown. No other poet of our time has written so many lines which delight the imagination and give us a sense of magical freedom. The marvellous

> Like Ethiopia ever jewelled bright

fills the mind, tranquillizes it as it is tranquillized by a vast and serene landscape. The more intimate

157

> with a sweet and velvet lip
> The snapdragons within the fire
> Of their red summer never tire,

takes us into the same delightful and tiny world as Donne's

> Thy little brethren, which like fairy sprites
> Oft skipp'd into our chamber, those sweet nights.

And more rarely, speaking of

> little marches all beribboned gay
> That lead down the lime avenues away,

Miss Sitwell has put the pathos of life into a few words.

But perhaps the passages in her poetry which give one the justest conception of her qualities are those in which the whole visible world appears as if it were suddenly fixed, a monstrous illusion. In this world where cheeks are like painted wood or round, hard fruits, humanity seems to lie in a heavy sleep, and is as securely subject to the vegetable processes of the earth as trees are. This vision of the world is original; there is nothing else like it. But applied as it is to the multitudes of people who spend their lives in unintelligible activity, it is not only original; it is true and profound. For these people, apparently so busy, making money, running about their affairs, are in one sense hardly alive at all. In the realms where the poet and the thinker move freely they are stationary, or if they stir their movements have the infinite slowness of a nightmare. To see humanity in this way is to see it fanatically, without proportion, without that feeling of solidarity with it which distinguishes humanistic poetry. But it is at the same time to see it intensely and unconditionally, and outside all our ordinary ways of seeing. There is an order of poetry—Blake and Rimbaud have adorned it —whose function is to show us the world in this way; and it is to this order that Miss Sitwell's poetry essentially belongs.

159

ROBERT GRAVES

~ X ~

ROBERT GRAVES

MR. GRAVES is one of the most puzzling figures in contemporary literature. He is conspicuously honest, yet he is often evasive; he is bold—and suddenly cautious; he is more dogmatic than any other contemporary poet, and perhaps more really sceptical at the same time. And it is in his poems of conflict that he is most sceptical, in his poems of escape that he is most daring. The best poems in *Country Sentiment,* which he describes himself as poems of escape, are admirably sincere; they face the reality of things more concretely than most of the later poetry, concerned with more everyday problems. Their sincerity, moreover, is of a very rare kind. For it takes far less courage, as modern psychology tells us, to face external realities than it takes to recognize the realities within us, especially when these are unconscious

163

realities becoming conscious, as they are in *Country Sentiment*. Like everybody else the poet must, of course, adapt himself to the world around him. To learn what one's environment is and to relate oneself to that is a utilitarian activity which cannot be avoided; but its attainment is not the work of poetry but of commonsense. Approaching reality directly in this way, we are working with the conscious mind on the raw fact; a harmony, therefore, cannot result, but only a compromise. Where Mr. Graves's poetry fails, as where a great deal of modern poetry fails, is where we have this bare confrontation of the conscious mind and the raw reality. The identity of the seer with the thing seen, the subjective-objective reality of vision, is not attained; this condition is only a stage towards its attainment; poetry in embryo, not poetry born. And though it is desirable that the modern world should find expression in poetry, that will never be done by one who sets out, in spite of his repugnance, to do so. It will only be done when a poet finds the modern world within himself, when not merely the outward, conscious adaptation to it has been made, but the inner, uncon-

164

scious one as well. This is, indeed, a platitude; yet a number of modern theories of poetry ignore it and dogmatize as if it were not there. Mr. Graves does not do so; his observations on the function and aim of poetry are always enlightened and often true; but his practice is tending less and less to conform to his best theory. In the second section of *Whipperginny* and in *Mock Beggar Hall* he has no longer the integral approach to the theme which we find in his earlier poetry. He no longer attacks the problem with all his faculties, finding a resolution on the various planes of the mind, as he has said poetry should; he attacks it only with his intellect, enlisting the imagination, if at all, as a supernumerary. He does not reveal convictions and intuitions; he treats general ideas which, we feel, have not been assimilated to his poetic nature and are perhaps alien to it. The will to adaptation is in his later work, rather than the living act of adaptation, and all that a will of this kind can give the poet is a compromise, not a reconciling vision of life, not a resolution.

And it is for a compromise that Mr. Graves

165

seems to be out in his later poetry and in his criticism. His criticism is very illuminating, both for what it says and for what it tells us about himself. He is an out-and-out relativist. What is good poetry to one man, he claims, is bad poetry to another; what this age finds significant a later one will find meaningless. Bad poetry is poetry which does not ease or clarify our subconscious conflicts; but it may ease or clarify the complexes of another generation, and then it will become good poetry. The theory is consistent, but so are most theories of criticism; the important thing is to find out what by means of it the author wishes to prove. For problems of this kind are never resolved; their terms are only changed from time to time by the action of fresh intelligences. In what way has Mr. Graves's candid and unconventional intelligence changed them? In two ways chiefly: by casting doubt on the supreme utterances of poetry (for no poetry can be supreme which is good in one age and bad in another); and by making the criterion of poetry very largely a utilitarian one. Nothing could show more clearly Mr. Graves's compromising temper. For when a man becomes convinced that compromise is essential he will in time come to prefer the second-best to the best, or at any rate the good to the surpassing, recognizing that for his purposes the former is the more effective. Moreover compromise and a utilitarian preoccupation go together, the criterion of every compromise being essentially its usefulness. There would be no point in controverting Mr. Graves's theories. They are a stimulating addition to critical thought; they emphasize factors which literary criticism almost always ignores, factors at present of the first importance. The question is whether Mr. Graves has emphasized them in the right way.

To take an extreme example, even if in certain ages Shakespeare has been a bad poet (not touching their particular conflicts), there is still a vast difference between him, in any age, and a bad poet like Martin Tupper. It is for differences as important as this that Mr. Graves's critical theory does not provide. The psychological effect of poetry is so important to him that as a theorist he has an eye for very little else. "For the poet," he says, "the writing of poetry accomplishes a certain end, irrespective of whether the poem ever finds another reader but himself; it enables him to be rid of the conflicts between his subpersonalities. And for the reader, the reading of poetry performs a similar service; it acts for him as a physician of his mental disorders." As far as it goes this is no doubt true; but the poet may rid himself of his subconscious conflicts in an infinity of ways, and on various planes, and as important as his release is the manner in which he effects it. For to rid oneself of a conflict is to be in a different state, and the quality of that state is not a matter of indifference. Yet to Mr. Graves sometimes it seems to be indifferent what the state is so long as the conflict has been removed. "Francis Thompson's *Sister Songs* and Lear's *Nonsense Rhymes*," he says, "are apparently the same sort of escape from the same sort of conflict; strange that Lear is treated less seriously. And who will say that the foolery in Edward Lear is less worthy of our tragic imagination than the terrible foolery at the crisis of *King Lear*?" The only thing that can be said in reply to this is that by the foolery

168

in *King Lear* our conflicts are released into an
infinitely greater world than they are by Edward
Lear's nonsense verses. Although both help to
rid us of our conflicts, they move us in completely different ways and with vastly different
power. Nonsense verse does give our conflicts a
certain relief. It presents us with a lively picture
of the utter unintelligibility of our subconscious
war, and the resignation to that unintelligibility
loosens our tensions for a time. The mood of
nonsense and the mood of mystery are alike in as
far as they are evoked by things which seem unintelligible; the great difference between them is
that while the one is a giving way to meaninglessness, the other is an attempt to impose meaning
upon it. Not even to the curative psychologist
concerned only to release the pressure of a conflict
in the subconscious mind could these modes of
relief appear of equal importance; to a poet interested in the positive temper of the soul it is quite
impossible to see how they can.

It is when we come to Mr. Graves's later poetry
that we see some of the bad effects of this curiously
pragmatic evaluation of the act of poetic expres-

169

sion. The change is decisively marked in *Whip-perginny,* and the preface to the volume tells us that the author was aware of it. The first part of the book, he says, continues the mood of *The Pier Glass,* "aggressive and disciplinary, rather than escapist." "But in most of the later pieces," he adds, "will be found evidences of greater detach-ment in the poet and the appearance of a new series of problems in religion, psychology and philosophy, no less exacting than their predeces-sors, but, it may be said, of less emotional in-tensity." In this later poetry and in some which Mr. Graves has written since, we are conscious that each poem is a theme chosen. We admire the manner in which the poet's mind deals with it; but subject and mind are not fused; and it is not an experience that is registered, but a hypoth-esis. Nor is that the worst, for we are often aware that the poetry is performing a set psycho-logical function. The machinery is too apparent. Certain of the poems in *Whipperginny—The Technique of Perfection,* for instance, and *The Bowl and the Rim*—are simply hypothetical statements of the general conditions of psychological conflict, about which the poet is clarifying his mind. But in resolving our subconscious conflicts poetry does not inform us of them, as psychoanalysis does; its operation is different; it takes place on the various planes of the psyche, and not, as in psycho-analysis, on the one which gives the key to the others; its effect is thus a harmonizing of the mind, rather than a clarifying of it. When Mr. Graves informs us in his poetry of the subconscious conflicts, therefore, he is forcing the natural growth of poetry with his intellect, and forcing it for a utilitarian purpose, that the effects of poetry might be enjoyed. In a process such as this the impulses of the unconscious are given a ready-made shape before they appear; the poet is prepared for them, and therefore against them, in advance; and the result is that they never achieve an organic expression, but only a schematized one. They are categories by the time Mr. Graves handles them, rather than energies. The only way one can mark the difference between

Across two counties he can hear,
And catch your words before you speak.
The woodlouse or the maggot's weak
Clamour rings in his sad ear,

from *The Pier Glass,* and

Let us live upright, yet with care consider
Whether, in living thus, we do not err,

from *Whipperginny,* is by saying that the first
contains potentially all that is in the second, and
contains as well something more. And when one
compares the much earlier *In the Wilderness* with
the recent *The Clipped Stater*, the discrepancy is
still greater. *In the Wilderness* is not one of Mr.
Graves's best poems, it is too inconclusive; but the
difference between

Basilisk, cockatrice,
Flocked to his homilies,
With mail of dread device,
With monstrous barbèd slings,
With eager dragon eyes;
Great rats on leather wings,
And poor blind broken things,
Foul in their miseries,

and

Then Finity is true Godhead's final test,
Nor does it shear the grandeur from Free Being;
"I must fulfil myself by self-destruction."
The curious phrase renews his conquering zest,

is definite and striking. It is the difference between a state imagined and a state hypothecated
and only dipped in the imagination to be given an
intellectual convincingness. The first passage
has the immediacy of psychological reality, the
second has not. It lacks the truth which we feel
in poetry when there is an organic correspondence
between the external image and the inner conflict
or desire—that correspondence which clamps
poetry to reality and gives it an absolute force.
The Clipped Stater is a floating fancy thrown off
by the inconstant mind; it has no necessity; it
may or may not be true. The question is not
whether *The Clipped Stater* is poetry. It is a
question rather of the relative value of two kinds
of work which Mr. Graves has produced and still
continues to produce side by side. In literary
criticism nothing can be proved; the only thing
that one can say is that by poetry like *In the
Wilderness* something is done that by *The Clipped*

173

Stater is not done at all; that the first is real, the second—not certainly so; that they are consequently of different worth.

The interesting thing about Mr. Graves is that with such an effective equipment for compromise he sometimes deserts it and leads an attack on his own defences. Nothing could be more different from the temporizing relativity of the critical books and the stifling compromise of *Mock Beggar Hall* than an occasional poem like *The Rock Below.* "Where speedwell grows and violets grow" the poet plucks up the flowers and finds stumps of thorn beneath. These come up and he sets a rose bush where they were.

> Love has pleasure in my roses
> For a summer space.

But the roots of the rose bush turn on stone, so he tears them up and far beneath strikes on the rock, "jarring hatefully." But "up the rock shall start."

> Now from the deep and frightful pit
> Shoots forth the spiring phœnix-tree
> Long despaired in this bleak land,

174

Holds the air with boughs, with bland
Fragrance welcome to the bee,
With fruits of immortality.

The contradiction in Mr. Graves's poetry is fundamental. On the one hand we have the consistent relativism of his later poetry, on the other, a determination to dig down until his mind produces "fruits of immortality." There is the mass of his busy, temporizing, hypothetical verse, verse which seems to say, "This may be true, or it may not"; there are a few poems which leave no room for the relative or for questions of this kind. *Lost Love* and *A Lover since Childhood* have this incontestable seriousness; some of the poems at the beginning of *Country Life* have it in a higher degree than any Mr. Graves has written since. In these, and still more clearly in poems like *In the Wilderness* and *The Rock Below*, Mr. Graves shows himself to be an original poet. In his later pseudo-philosophical poetry the thought, while lively and full of idiosyncrasy, is never very original; the supposititious form in which it is advanced makes it appear far more profound than it is in reality. It may be that Mr. Graves's excursion into philosophy will deepen his mind, and that later he will return with fuller powers to the kind of poetry which he seems so inevitably equipped to write. Meanwhile one can only note the passing phase.

CONTEMPORARY POETRY

~ XI ~

CONTEMPORARY POETRY

To disengage the qualities and estimate the rank of the poetry of one's generation is peculiarly difficult. In the first place the qualities which the critic has to discern (seeing that he, too, is of the age) are in a sense his own, and cannot be seen objectively; and secondly, it is impossible for him to separate his reactions to them from the rank of the poetry which they distinguish. A third thing will influence his judgment: the quantity of contemporary poetry. There is very little poetry being written to-day, and it is legitimate criticism to note that by its nature it is not poetry that could be produced in great quantity. It is the kind of poetry which is written in an age of general poetic debility, which is achieved against the current, caught adroitly where it can be caught, or seized desperately in the midst of hostile forces. It has the qualities of a thing which must use its wits: it is stubborn, violent, or clever. In the Victorian age poetry held its own: in the Romantic era it was supreme and even the prose writers were dominated by it. But to find another age in which the genius of prose was so immensely more powerful than that of poetry as it is now, we have to go back to the eighteenth century.

That century was the century of enlightenment; our age, too, is one of enlightenment, but on a far vaster scale. The genius of our generation, as Mr. Bertrand Russell has said, has gone into science, not into literature. And it seems to be a fact of experience that to the supremely creative, the poetic, power, the spirit of enlightenment, when it is widely disseminated, becomes inimical. Science, enlightenment, scepticism,—these make us look coldly, and involuntarily, automatically so, upon the things which the poet must contemplate with passion. The theorist's impersonality of intellect becomes insensibly an impersonality of general habit, and eventually an impersonality of feeling. We have all been influenced by the theories of science, and the intellectualization of

180

imaginative literature has been going on for a long time. It produced in the generation before last such things as the dissolvent plays of Ibsen, and, perhaps its most finished expression, the "pity" of Anatole France, so admirable in the man, so inadequate in the artist. For France did not pity the immediate object, nor even pity in him the human race; he pitied humanity directly, passing by the particular case in indicating it, making it an open occasion for a quite impersonal emotion of which it only served to remind him, but which it did not intensify. The pity of France is not typical of this age, but his impersonality is; our emotions are colder, more generalized, more intelligent perhaps, than they were fifty years ago.

The growth and dissemination of science has made our approach to experience more impersonal; the circumstances of modern life tend to do the same thing. No one has investigated properly the effect of the growth of cities upon literature, politics, and popular conceptions of morality. Yet the effect of such a vast change must have been great. It is impossible, for example, to conceive a poem like *The Waste Land* being written anywhere except in a huge modern city; the small, dirty, leisurely London of fifty years ago did not contain the atmosphere for it. The atmosphere was not there, but neither was any way of life, any class of experience, which could make such utterance as this comprehensible. As we read *The Waste Land* modern London, though not deliberately evoked, seems to rise up around us like a wall. Miss Sitwell's poetry, too, recalls us to London, and if we except that of Mr. Squire's followers, there is hardly any poetry of the present day which does not do so. In the main, English poetry has been a poetry of the English country; it is now a poetry chiefly of the town. This is a decisive change. But it is also a comprehensible and natural one; for the cities are alive, the countryside is no longer so.

The effects of this vast change in the life of England must needs be infinitely complex, and finally impossible to define. The most one can do is to take hold of a few generalizations, obvious enough when stated, and yet, perhaps, generally overlooked. In the first place, life in a large city is necessarily more impersonal than life in the country. The difference, indeed, is so great that anybody coming to the city from the country has to re-orient his values or else remain permanently at a loss. Where formerly his contacts were all personal, here he finds that they are preponderantly collective. His circle of acquaintances has been superseded by a crowd, permanent but shifting, as much a part of the furniture of the streets as the houses and shops. For the individual has been substituted the mass, and to the mass the order of feelings which expressed his relations towards his circle of acquaintances is no longer relevant. He develops, therefore, another set, the peculiar set of impersonal feelings which all town-bred people carry about with them, without guessing it, from their birth, the feelings which seem to make them a part of the crowd and yet keep them outside it, which permit them to know it and yet ignore it. Everything, moreover, is on such a large scale, business, the populace, the machinery of life, that nothing seems to matter so much. A calamity is one in a series of calamities; a man is part of a crowd. In the last hundred years England in general has come from the country to the city; the city as we know it, moreover, is like nothing which the human race has seen before: these attitudes, these emotions, are therefore new. They were bound to influence thought and feeling, and to bring a different note into literature.

Still another thing has helped to change the atmosphere of England, and to change it subversively: the rapidity of change. In a stable order of society, or in solitude, men may listen to their feelings without much question, for these feelings correspond to the situation; they have a sort of suitability. But where change is very rapid our reactions tend to become obsolete before we realize it. True of a past in which we always tend to live, the present delights in refuting them. They become confused, lose their force, and cease to give us satisfaction, as soon as we see that another set of responses, which, however, we cannot command, would be more suitable. So it was inevitable that we should have in contemporary literature a general distrust of the feelings, a conditional or ironical presentation of them, and sometimes a frank reduction of them to their lowest factors: to those elements which men never

184

distrust even when they distrust everything else.

These things, then, must be taken into account when we consider contemporary literature, for they are part of our environment, and the creative writer lives not in a world of poetry but in his environment. If poetry is colder, more intellectualized, more sceptical, than it used to be, this, we see, is a natural result of the fact that contemporary thought and life impose upon us an increasingly impersonal attitude. If poetry is conditional and ironical, affirming and denying in one breath, what response could be more natural to a world which has changed so rapidly that no one knows where he stands? And these attributes of modern poetry become more significant if we see them neither as qualities assumed, nor as a fashion, nor as a new approach to reality, but as a reaction, genuine if confused, to the world we know. The poetry of Mr. Eliot, Miss Sitwell and Mr. Graves, seen thus, is a poetry congruous with the nature of the age. It is neither a complete criticism nor a fulfilment; for that we are still waiting. But the age makes it comprehensible, gives it validity; we see clearly in it the

forces which mould and the obstacles which in-
hibit modern life.

Let us take the testimony of the poets themselves. Miss Sitwell has a few very frank and
illuminating notes in *Bucolic Comedies*. "We
are accused of triviality; but poetry is no longer
a just and terrible Judgment Day—a world of
remorseless and clear light." "Modern heart-
break is merely a dulling and a retrogression, a
travelling backward: till man is no longer the
bastard of beasts and of gods, but is blind, eye-
less, shapeless as the eternal stones, or exists with
the half-sentience of the vegetable world—a
sentience that is so intensely concerned with the
material world (as apart from the visual) that it
is like the sentience of the blind." "This modern
world is but a thin match-board flooring spread
over a shallow hell. For Dante's hell has faded,
is dead. Hell has no vastness; there are no more
devils who laugh or who weep—only the maimed
dwarfs of life, terrible straining mechanisms,
crouching on trivial sands, and laughing at the
giants crumbling!"

Let us turn to Mr. Eliot. "I have lost my passion," says Gerontion,

> I have lost my passion; why should I need to keep it
> Since what is kept must be adulterated?

and the queries go on through Mr. Eliot's poetry:

> Who clipped the lion's wings
> And flea'd his rump and pared his claws?

> Where is the penny world I bought
> To eat with Pipit behind the screen? . . .
> Where are the eagles and the trumpets?

> What are the roots that clutch, what branches grow
> Out of this stony rubbish?

> What shall we do to-morrow?
> What shall we ever do? The hot water at ten.
> And if it rains, a closed car at four.

And with that finality which Mr. Eliot can communicate over such a keen undertone of rebellion:

> I have heard the key
> Turn in the door once and turn once only.

It is the same cry as Miss Sitwell's. The "giants crumbling"—the lion with the clipped wings and flea'd rump; the "trivial sands"—the "stony rubbish"; the hell with "no vastness"—the "penny world"; the sentience that is like "the sentience of the blind"—the key turned in the door once and turned once only: these are images of one and the same world, the modern world which has risen silently around us, and in which we have not learned to think and to feel.

The response of the poet to this world is not pessimism, for pessimism is a reasonable and traditional thing; it is rather a bewilderment and distress of mind. The poet is not concerned because ideals do not correspond to realities (a great source of pessimistic poetry); he is hardly concerned with ideals at all. His bewilderment springs from something far more complex: the feeling that reality itself has broken down, that even the simple emotions, the instinctive reactions, are disorientated and lead us astray. This bewilderment has not the absoluteness of pessimism, but it is nevertheless more completely without consolations.

There is a satisfaction in making an end of the matter and saying, like Leopardi:

> *Non val cosa nessuna*
> *I moti tuoi; e fango è il mondo.*

But the contemporary poet is not so sure that "the world is mud"; he does not know, indeed, what it is; for if even the physical reactions appear doubtful, anything may be true. The suffering which is reflected in his poetry is, therefore, the suffering of uncertainty, which, unlike all other kinds of suffering, has no power to distil its own alleviation. To him the miseries of the world are not even misery; for he cannot give them a meaning, or find a place for them in human life. Everything is conditional, everything is potential. Modern thought and modern life present the poet with a number of possible worlds, but not with the one which he needs if he is to feel, as well as speculate upon, reality. His temptation in this quandary is to accept these possible worlds provisionally, and build fanciful hypotheses round them.

189

This is what Mr. Graves has done in his later poetry. Miss Sitwell and Mr. Eliot describe the bewilderment and misery of the mind surrounded by uncertainty; Mr. Graves, too, has described that bewilderment and misery, but he has turned more and more of late years to a poetry whose chief implication is that anything may be true. It is a highly theoretical, very laborious, and intellectually serious, poetry of escape; and it is difficult to see what other kind of poetry the age presented to a poet with a philosophical turn. Donne, as Professor Grierson points out, "was in the first place a Catholic" and had moreover "a vast and growing store of the same scholastic learning, the same Catholic theology, as controlled Dante's thought, but jostling already with the new learning of Copernicus and Paracelsus." With that new learning Donne furnished the scholastic, Catholic mansion anew, transforming it so that from the inside at any rate it seemed something completely novel; yet the original edifice remained. But Mr. Graves, in whose mind the theories of Professor Freud, Dr. Rivers, Butler and Sir James G. Frazer jostle one another,

has no cosmos in which to assemble them; the
age provides none, and it is the lack of a frame-
work of reality which makes his fancies remain
merely fancies where Donne's are as concrete as
ornaments on a great design. It is this that
makes us feel when Mr. Graves describes the
transmigration of Alexander the Great's soul into
the body of a Chinese soldier that it is a mere
hypothesis, whereas Donne's fantasy of the soul's
transit to Heaven is pure passion and imagination:

> Who if she meet the body of the sun,
> Goes through, not waiting till his course be run;
> Who finds in Mars his camp no corps of guard,
> Nor is by Jove, nor by his father barr'd;
> But ere she can consider how she went,
> At once is at, and through the firmament.

What makes this passage of almost absurd fancy
so moving, so serious, is Donne's absolute acceptance of the premises from which he starts.
Without an unconditional belief in the immortality of the soul, and in time and eternity as its
two states, poetry such as this could not be written. It is, then, the lack of any metaphysical

foundations to Mr. Graves's fancies which makes them sometimes so singularly cold, so unconvincing.

> Why might we not approve adulterous license
> Increasing pleasurable experience?
> What could the soul lose through the body's rapture
> With a body not its mate, where thought is pure?

The difference between the poetry of Donne and poetry such as this is the difference between absolute and conditional utterance, between what is true and what may or may not be true, between the poetry of a man living in a real world and that of one torn between several hypothetical ones, none of them acceptable. Donne's hypotheses started from problems which he had resolved by experience or by faith; Mr. Graves's start from this premise or that, and in general from the unresolved problems of the age. Poetry of this kind may be witty, ironical, or suggestive, but it is not serious enough for its purpose, it is not effectual. For the pressing need of any age of transition is to cease to be one, to attain to a resolution of its problems, not to poetize them.

We have a host of theories, then, but among

192

them no ruling theory; a mass of enlightenment, but no faith in enlightenment; a number of ideals of society, but no hope that they will be realized. The world has changed around us, but we are not conscious of having changed it; and the future is still more uncertain than the present. We have lost, in other words, the things which in a period of transition are always lost, but which with its passing return again, somewhat changed by the fact that it has happened. Among these are such conceptions as the cosmos, society, humanity, a general purpose, and, as an inevitable expression of these, such literary categories as the tragic, the pathetic, the comic. The present dislike for "the pathetic fallacy" and for *catharsis* is peculiar to a society which is not integrated. Once postulate a great order and these things become inevitable, for any enduring belief, the belief of a civilization in God, in humanity, or in itself, makes certain things pathetic and tragic, giving its meaning naturally and involuntarily to the varied accidents of life. Ages of transition cannot give this significance to the accidents of their existence; in them accordingly the peculiarly significant cate-

193

gories of literature are questioned or are denied.
Yet if we could write in the great pathetic vein,
we should not question the validity of pathos; if
we could attain to a catharsis, our doubts about
its desirability would be resolved. We live in an
interregnum, between a world which has passed
and one not born: not in a new order, but rather
in the chaos where a new order must be preparing.
For if civilized societies change they also tend
perpetually to reintegrate themselves; at its moment the stable order of life and thought, better or
worse than its preceding type, returns.

The service of a period of transition is to make
us conscious of the problems which the dead order
could not solve. These problems accumulate; the
old order thrusts them aside, goes on as long as it
can as if they did not exist. Then the crash
comes; the order no longer is there; the problems,
these and these alone, fill our minds. There is
hardly an aspect of life, hardly a feeling or a general conception, which the universal questioning of
our age has left untouched; and when order rises
again we feel that everything will be changed.
The progress of industrialism and the growth of

cities have modified our feelings, our relations, our desires. The discoveries and theories of science have altered our conception of the nature of life, and of the origin and destiny of mankind and of the world. With these revolutions the last great era of literature, the Victorian, could do little. Nor can we do very much with them, for we are not so much conscious of them as of the universal uncertainty into which they plunge everything. Yet gradually that uncertainty must resolve into something else, which will not be a dogma, nor a theory, but a living complex of beliefs, experiences, acceptances; a new adaptation. The universe of science will then become real; we will recognize it not merely as intellectually valid, but as the actual universe in which we live. "If the time should come," Wordsworth says, "when what is now called science, thus familiarized to men, shall be ready to put on, as it were, a form of flesh and blood, the poet will lend his divine spirit to aid the transfiguration, and will welcome the being thus produced as a dear and genuine inmate of the household of man." The poet will do so because nothing is wholly real until it finds an

image as well as a formula for itself. For the
image is the record that a conception has been
steeped in the unconscious, and there accepted by
the deeper potencies of the mind. Because it was
once accepted in this way the cosmogony of the
Bible is still in one sense more real than that of
modern science; for while we no longer accept it,
we cannot but visualize it. God creating the
world in seven days, "making" Adam and Eve
and the animals and fishes, setting Heaven above
us and Hell beneath, calling the world to account
on the Day of Judgment: these are still as vivid as
dreams, because once for a long time they had
such reality that men could see them as if they
were happening before their eyes. It is the
measure of the mere intellectuality of the evolu-
tionary theory of creation that it has never become a picture. It is hypothesis, not imaginative
reality. Yet "the remotest discoveries of the
Chemist, the Botanist, the Mineralogist," to quote
Wordsworth again, "will be as proper objects of
the poet's art as any upon which it can be em-
ployed, if the time should ever come when these
shall be familiar to us, and the relations under

which they are contemplated by the followers of
these respective sciences shall be manifestly and
palpably material to us as enjoying and suffering beings." The discoveries of modern science
are certainly "material to us as enjoying and suffering beings." They have revolutionized our
conception of the three problems which chiefly
concern poetry and mankind: the problems of
creation, destiny and the nature of life: how we
came to be, whither we go, and what we are.
The reason why the poet has not taken these discoveries as the objects of his art can only be because they are not really familiar to him, because
while he accepts them intellectually, his unconscious has not accepted them.

If all this is so, there need be no wonder that
poetry to-day is hard to write. Living in a world
intellectually formulated the poet has to make it
into a real one. His task is thus not so much to
treat the universe of life as to evoke it. That
world will some time be evoked; the universe of
science will become as real to us as the universe
of the Bible was to our predecessors; the geologic
ages, the dragons before the Flood, our first an-

cestors—these will become "genuine inmates of the household of man." They have already been absorbed into the science of psychology; they will be absorbed into poetry because they must, because until they are they will not be humanized, and because if they are not humanized they will remain a remnant of defeated experience. There have been a few magnificent but abortive attempts to absorb them, the greatest of these *Also Sprach Zarathustra,* with its new table of values, its acceptance of a world not anthropomorphic, its use of mythological material, its profound recognition of the unconscious, which forestalled so strikingly the later attitude of psycho-analysis. The universe to which Nietzsche tried to orient himself was indeed the universe which modern knowledge had revealed, but he rarely reached past a will-to-acceptance to acceptance itself. Yet we cannot feel that he failed because he came too soon. The fault lay rather within himself; his inspiration as a poet was impure, like Shelley's. The resolution of the modern world into poetry might, one feels, have been achieved by him had his fanaticism and his ambition been less. The

198

time was ripe, if he had been. As it is, the work of resolution has still to be done. When it is done the condition of a new productive era will be in existence.

CONTEMPORARY FICTION

CONTEMPORARY FICTION

LAMENTING in *The Common Reader* the absence of authoritative criticism, Mrs. Woolf draws a picture of the contemporary writer producing his work "with infinite pains and in almost utter darkness." The phrase no doubt describes the state of a great number of writers at present, and almost certainly of the few who can be taken seriously. This state was inevitable, the age being what it is; for we live in an era of transition, and in eras of transition writers are all half-blind to one another: the magic convention, the wished-for order which would set them in clear light, refuses to be evoked. To understand one's age is to understand oneself, to give oneself direction and a sort of self-evident validity. The ages which permitted this understanding, such ages as the Elizabethan and the Johnsonian, increased

203

the writer's faith in himself, allied themselves
with what was productive in him, and generally
made his path clear as nothing else could have
done. They were ages in which certain orders of
values were accepted, ages which had an image
of the cosmos, society, morality, humanity, destiny,
of what was wise and desirable, possible and impossible. The writer did not necessarily accept
this order, but because it was an order every conviction, every influence emanating from it, tended
to make him more comprehensible to himself.
Living in an intelligible world he had to render
his qualities coherent, to relate them to each other,
to complete them. In ages of transition, on the
other hand, everything makes the writer more uncertain, saps his faith, only nourished from himself, and gives his work an air either of vacilla-
tion or of violence. His achievement may be
sometimes remarkable, but always it will be
partial. He will be a writer with one quality or
with a few, but he will not have the complete ar-
ray of qualities, each depending upon and imply-
ing the others, which a unified conception of life
imposes. If we are to understand contemporary

literature, and especially that part of it which most immediately mirrors the time, it is necessary to start from the hypothesis that we live in an age of transition. The qualities of the contemporary novel, its particular approach to life, its defects and virtues, are the qualities, the virtues and defects, of an age of transition.

So if we take the work of our most representative novelists, of Mr. Joyce, Mr. Lawrence, Mrs. Woolf, Mr. Stephen Hudson, Mr. Aldous Huxley, we will find that a common note distinguishes it. That note is first and most obviously the note of originality; the critic can point to no other age which has been so original in method and in intention. The writers mentioned above have sought to bring new provinces of experience into fiction, and in general have experimented with language and forms. Their attitude is essentially different from that of Fielding and Thackeray setting out to paint a picture of society, or Dickens and Scott telling a human tale. To writers such as these the words which Mr. W. B. Yeats uses of the traditional artist may be applied. "Corneille and Racine," he says, "did not deny their masters.

. . . In their day imitation was conscious or all but conscious, and because originality was but so much more a part of the man himself, so much the deeper because unconscious, no quick analysis could unravel their miracle, that needed generations, it may be, for its understanding; but it is our imitation that is unconscious and that waits the certainties of time."

This is true, certainly, of writers living in a great order. The convention for the *grand siècle* had been found; imitation, therefore, was a useful practice, indeed, a necessary measure. Yet how irrelevant Mr. Yeats's words seem to us; how little we feel their truth. For the essential characteristic of an era of transition is that the old conventions no longer work, and that the new one has not been found; the imitation which once gave the writer the free entry to his world has become meaningless. Scott and Dickens, Thackeray and George Eliot, were not concerned with questions of method. They had no need to be; they lived in a settled order and they used a well-tried convention perfectly suited to express it. Their originality was therefore "but so much more

a part of the man himself, so much the deeper
because unconscious." But in an age without
living models originality becomes primary; it is
not the personal accentuation of a common idiom;
it is personal first and last of all. And in being
that it becomes, indeed, something more: an unconscious attempt to find a way out of the chaos,
to discover a convention and found an order.
Originality of this kind is in the highest degree
useful. For in a general absence of values any
writer's truth may be valid; what is true to him
may become true to others; it is well therefore
that everything possible should be said. So
when Mr. Joyce, Mr. Lawrence, Mrs. Woolf, and
Mr. Hudson strike out new paths, they are not
only doing what the age compels every serious
writer to do; they are carrying out the task it imposes upon them. The diversity of their responses may for a time add to the confusion; but
that is an inconvenience incident on any attempt
to bring order out of chaos. To think oneself
down into experience and then record one's conclusions without too much regard for conventions past or potential, is the best that any

writer can do in an age such as ours. It is because Mr. Joyce has done this with such extraordinary integrity that *Ulysses*, in spite of its many defects, is so important and so comprehensively revolutionary.

But though in an age of transition all the writers speak as if no one else were speaking and hardly anybody listening, what they say has of necessity a resemblance. In eras of order similarity of thought is openly accepted; in ages of transition it is unconscious. Contemporary fiction accordingly shows us not merely isolated voices, but tones, tendencies, which become clearer when we compare ourselves with other ages. Perhaps the strongest of these is the tendency to reduce all the manifestations of the human consciousness, all human relations, emotions, thoughts, to their elements. Every reality which is not physiological is now sceptically analysed into something else. The traditional, which is to say the distinctively human, conceptions of such things as love, friendship, honour, duty, are not accepted as obvious realities. What gives *Ulysses* the peculiar impress of the age is not so

much that it is full of experiments in form as that
there is in it no real attempt to portray realities
of this order. Nor does Mr. Huxley deal with
them. Mr. Lawrence does, but he reduces them
to their elements, to realities, certainly, but not to
peculiarly human realities. Mr. Hudson admits
them, but with a note of interrogation. These
are four representative names; but a great number of lesser ones could be added to them. To
feel in this way, then, is not the idiosyncrasy of
an isolated writer; it is fairly general; and there
has been nothing like it before in English fiction.
Fielding, Smollett, Thackeray, Jane Austen,—all
these saw clearly enough the lust and egotism
of mankind; but they never doubted that love,
selfish as it might be, had an existence as objective
as appetite, or that friendship, however rare, was
any more to be gainsaid than what often mas-
querades under its name. Nor have such things
been doubted by recent writers like Mr. Bennett
and Mr. Wells.

To understand how this attitude came to be we
have to go back to Ibsen, Nietzsche and Mr.
Shaw, dissimilar as these are in spirit from the

writers of our time. For it was Ibsen who first effectually began to question all the ratified human attitudes, honour, the ties of blood, the relations between the sexes; he questioned them in the belief that if falsehood could be swept away humanity would build on truer foundations. Nietzsche questioned even more comprehensively, indicting virtue, kindness, reverence, altruism, but with a lofty belief in his work. Mr. Shaw attacked more particularly the romantic ideal of love, regarding it as a superstition which retarded mankind. The astonishing thing is that these attacks, as we can see now, have been to a large extent successful. Ibsen and Nietzsche questioned the human sentiments; Mr. Joyce and Mr. Huxley do so no longer; they simply treat them as things in which it would be stupid to believe. The destructive part of the work of the free intelligence of the last half-century has been successful; the hopes which were founded on its success have faded away. Nietzsche's Uebermensch, Ibsen's nations of noblemen, Shaw's vehicles of the Life Force; these we believe in no longer; and if we are beyond good and evil we have not found the kingdom that is there. This is the stage in the tragi-comedy of modern thought which has been reached by our generation.

In reaching it a great deal clearly has been lost; let us try to discover what has been gained. Chiefly, perhaps, a sense of the questionableness of the most simple emotions, the most sanctioned relations, the most stereotyped experiences. If love is not love, but a number of things concealed under a name; if all our feelings, actions, thoughts, are of the same nature; obviously the opportunity of experience is immensely widened, the whole view of the writer enlarged if for the moment confused. And in complexity, in meaning under meaning, the novel is richer now than it has ever been before. Certain writers, it is true, have used the weapon of analysis to simplify experience rather than enrich it. Mr. Huxley reduces the emotion not to the almost infinite number of elements which constitute it, but to one; and having done so, he discovers that it is far less interesting than the emotion itself. But the main tendency, in the novels of Mr. Joyce, Mrs. Woolf, Mr. Lawrence, is to reveal the in-

211

finite complexity which one experience, one emotion, may hold.

This process implies a disintegrating analysis. That disintegration has been carried far by Mr. Joyce, and it has been reintegrated by him once, but once only, in the figure of Mr. Bloom. For contemporary literature Mr. Bloom is accordingly a figure of supreme interest. He is not only a great character; he is a character in a new style. He is made up not of large and recognizable attributes, as most characters are, but of elements so minute that we cannot credit them to this or that class of moral experience. And precisely because they are of an order on which our moral sense, occupied with recognizable, practical and not subtle things, does not habitually operate, Mr. Bloom is more truly than any other figure in modern literature beyond good and evil. We apprehend him, that is to say, not only more minutely and encyclopædically than other imaginary figures; we apprehend in him the things which have no repercussion on his environment, which are silent to everybody and everything in the world but himself, which are part of him not as a man acting, speaking and suffering, but part rather of his sealed personality. It is this that makes us feel sometimes that so many things have been packed into Mr. Bloom that he is more than life size. In a newly created figure this is a very good sign; it shows that our consciousness of life has been enlarged. Mr. Bloom demonstrates in general, then, what fine effects may be got by assembling anew the particles of personality which the modern mind has separated and dispersed. He is the result of a new assemblage of elements, and his creation is less to be compared to an act of reproduction than one of incarnation.

But if Mr. Bloom is the most truly prophetic figure in contemporary literature, he typifies the failure of the modern spirit as well as its triumph. His solidity, his extension, are admirable; we "can walk round him." But we walk round him as we might walk round a colossal statue, or an inexhaustibly interesting effigy in a wax-works. For though he lets us see all his mind, he does not really respond to us; he is secret and silent, existing among the other characters as the gods exist among mortals in the Greek tales. In *Ulysses*,

213

while the characterization of the separate figures
is intimate, while these figures are interesting
within the bounds of their egos, they are immobile
towards each other; they have no intimate relationships. Between Mr. Joyce's men and women
there is a sexual understanding, and among his
men a masonic understanding; but that is all.
They are isolated figures, whose reaction is to the
mass, not to the individual; who live not in a society or in a circle of friends, but in the street;
who while acknowledging bonds have never built
up relationships to make these humanly endur-
able: The disintegration of all thought, sentiment, faith, is here carried to its conclusion. The
individual exists in a void. Everything has been
pulled down; nothing has been built up again except Mr. Bloom's lonely personality.

The point is important, for *Ulysses* is typical.
In Mr. Huxley's novels, too, the relations between
the characters are quite impersonal. The frankness of confession is great, but that is because
there is no real frankness of communication.
The characters are nothing to each other; therefore they can say what they like; it makes no

difference; and to be frank in this way is, indeed, a form of misanthropy. Mr. Lawrence has recognized the danger of this impotence to communicate. He began with the conviction that personal relationships were supremely important and in the modern world supremely difficult to attain; and he tried to break through to them by violence. He has been concerned with them ever since. But his perception of the difficulty of attaining them has driven him into the same isolation as that into which quite a different influence drove Mr. Joyce. Mr. Hudson has been chiefly occupied in describing the effects of false relationships, and in seeking the moral bases of real ones. His purpose is the same as Ibsen's; but he does not so much accept Ibsen's analysis as work in the same spirit. Mrs. Woolf alone, perhaps, has kept intact her sense of the reality of communication. She may analyse the traditional emotions and relations, but they remain real to her, like the air we breathe. It is this that makes her characters more intimate than those of Mr. Lawrence or Mr. Joyce. We are sorry to leave them, because a communication has been established between

them and us. The author's analysis has been
applied to them, but it only makes them more contemporary, more real. Mrs. Woolf has retained
the tradition of humanism, and by permeating it
with the new spirit has revivified it.

Nevertheless the general tendency of the novel
at present might be described as anti-humanistic.
To analyse the character into elements which seem
more real than it, is at first to dehumanize it, as
the physiologist at first dehumanizes the body for
us by drawing our attention to the separate organs,
each with an independent life of its own, and none
with a life we can understand. Later, when we
have got over the shock, we may have a more
noble conception of the economy of the body, and
realize that after all it is the supreme entity.
So in contemporary literature, when we have survived the shocks which the discoveries of our
analysis give us, the complete economy of the
mind will once more arise. The dispersion of
character, the drawing up of apparent irrelevancies from the subconscious, will bring us back to
the supreme entity, the soul, the mind, the self,
whatever we may call it, but with that reality

changed.   If a writer could humanize the stuff on which Mr. Joyce works, as the traditional artist humanized all the evil he knew, the humanistic tradition would be marvellously deepened.

And clearly there is only one way of humanizing that: it must be integrated in human characters and in a complex of human life, until it is made something corresponding completely to the network of feelings and relations amid which people live at present.   Mr. Joyce has given us a marvellous character in new style; the problem is to set that character in motion.   In doing that the novelist will have to marshal a far greater body of material than he does now; and his effects will be correspondingly more complex.   But there will be a principle of unity in his work then, which will make its complexity more really comprehensible than the half-and-half complexity of the contemporary novel.   For to set Mr. Bloom in motion, to place him in relation to figures as complex as himself, will be to create that new world which is only a vague, unrealized background to the contemporary novel.   That world, when it is realized, will be a very different one from any the past can show us. For the literature of transition, unsatisfying as it is, has brought new possibilities of the mind to light, has made certain things conscious which before were unconscious; and no novelist will be able in future to write as if that literature had never existed. In that lies its abundant justification.